THE SERIES™

AUTHENTIC™ MANHOOD

TRAINING GUIDE

A **MAN** AND HIS **TRAPS**

A **MAN** AND HIS **TRAPS**

Published by Authentic Manhood • • Reprinted 2019

ISBN 978-1-4158-7796-8 • Item 005558734

Project Management & Art Direction: Rachel Lindholm and Lindsey Woodward
Design: Samantha Corcoran, Mike Robinson, Details Communications
Editors: Rick Caldwell, Grant Edwards, Rachel Lindholm, Steve Snider, Rebekah Wallace, Lindsey Woodward
Contributors: John Bryson, Bryan Carter, Guy Delcambre, Grant Edwards, Tierce Green, Craig Gross, Grant Guffin, Traylor Lavvon, Steve Snider

To order additional copies of this resource, go to AuthenticManhood.com, contact LifeWay Resources online at LifeWay.com, or visit the LifeWay Christian Store serving you.

Printed in the United States of America

Distributed by:

Authentic Manhood
12115 Hinson Road, Suite 200
Little Rock, AR 72212

Groups Ministry Publishing
LifeWay Resources
One LifeWay Plaza
Nashville, TN 37234

TABLE of CONTENTS

How to **Experience** 33 as an **Individual** or **Group**

33 The Series can be viewed on DVD, downloaded from **authenticmanhood.com**, or experienced via mobile apps. Any of these three delivery systems can be utilized by groups or individuals. ***One of the great things about this series is the variety of ways it can be used and/or presented.***

The series is organized in a way that provides flexibility and offers a variety of options on how the material can be experienced. *33* is organized into six topically-themed volumes that include six sessions each. ***Volumes include topics on a man's design, story, traps, parenting, marriage, and career.*** You can choose to commit to one volume/topic at a time, by limiting a particular experience to six sessions, or you can combine multiple volumes into one expanded experience that includes more sessions (12, 18, 24, 30, or 36). You can also choose any combination thereof.

However you choose to experience 33, the manhood principles and practical insights taught in each volume are essential for every man on the journey to Authentic Manhood.

The Importance of Being in a **Community of Men**

Climbing a mountain alone is a difficult and even dangerous undertaking. Attempting to climb the mountain of manhood alone is also not recommended. Just like a mountain climber needs to belay or connect with another man for safety and support, we need other men around us to help us stay on course with our manhood.

Having other men deeply connected to us becomes invaluable when we slip, struggle, or stray off course in our manhood journey.

To fully enjoy 33, experience it in community with other men. The goal of this study is not just to fill in the blanks of your **Training Guide,** but also to fill in the blanks of your life. Having other men walk through the experience with you is key to moving this material from the pages of your **Training Guide** to the pages of your life.

MANHOOD COMMUNITY

1. **Provides encouragement.** Every man needs other men cheering for him and encouraging him on his journey to Authentic Manhood.
2. **Gives you additional insight.** Having other men around you helps you get a much better perspective on your life. Others can help you discover your blind spots and avoid costly mistakes.
3. **Brings constructive criticism.** We all need men in our lives who will be honest with us to help us become better men.
4. **Makes your journey richer.** Sharing life with a community of men makes the great times feel like a celebration and provides much needed support when life gets rough.

No one can force you to open up your life and work to make a connection with another man. Although it can be challenging and frightening, it is well worth the risk. 33

INTRO

From a **Weekly Gathering** to a **Global Movement**

Several years ago, Dr. Robert Lewis responded to the desire of a handful of men who were hungering for more than a Bible study. They wanted a map for manhood—a definition of what it meant to be a man. They needed help to leap over the hurdles they were encountering in life.

Robert responded by launching a weekly gathering called Men's Fraternity, challenging men to join him at six o'clock each Wednesday morning for 24-weeks. From the depth of his own personal experience and the pages of Scripture, Robert developed what came to be known as the Men's Fraternity series:

- *The Quest for Authentic Manhood*
- *Winning at Work & Home*
- *The Great Adventure*

What began with a few men huddling up grew into a weekly gathering of more than 300 men. In just a few years, local attendance at Men's Fraternity climbed to more than a 1000 men.

The message of Authentic Manhood began to spread and soon exploded into a global movement ***impacting more than a million men in more than 20,000 locations worldwide***—from locker rooms to boardrooms, from churches to prisons, on military bases and the field of battle, at NASA, and even on a space shuttle mission. Wherever the messages were heard, the challenge remained the same: to call men to step up and follow biblical manhood modeled by Jesus Christ.

The Men's Fraternity curriculum ***was created on the front lines where men live, written in the trenches in response to men who pleaded for purpose and direction.*** It has proven to be the most widely used and effective material on Authentic Manhood available today.

What began as a weekly meeting of men searching for answers to their manhood questions has grown into a bold movement that has dramatically impacted the lives of men, their families, and communities.

A Movement that **Grows Authentic Men** and **Plants Churches**

For over a decade, Fellowship Associates has helped more than ***a million men all over the world to discover the life of truth, passion, and purpose they were created to live through Authentic Manhood materials***. During that same decade, Fellowship Associates has been directing a church planting residency program that has been recognized as one of the most effective church planting efforts in the world.

The proceeds from the sale of Authentic Manhood materials have helped underwrite the planting of 56 (and growing) strategic churches throughout the United States as well as in Canada, Hong Kong, Dubai, Guatemala, Poland, and Spain.

~ Map of U.S. Church Plants ~

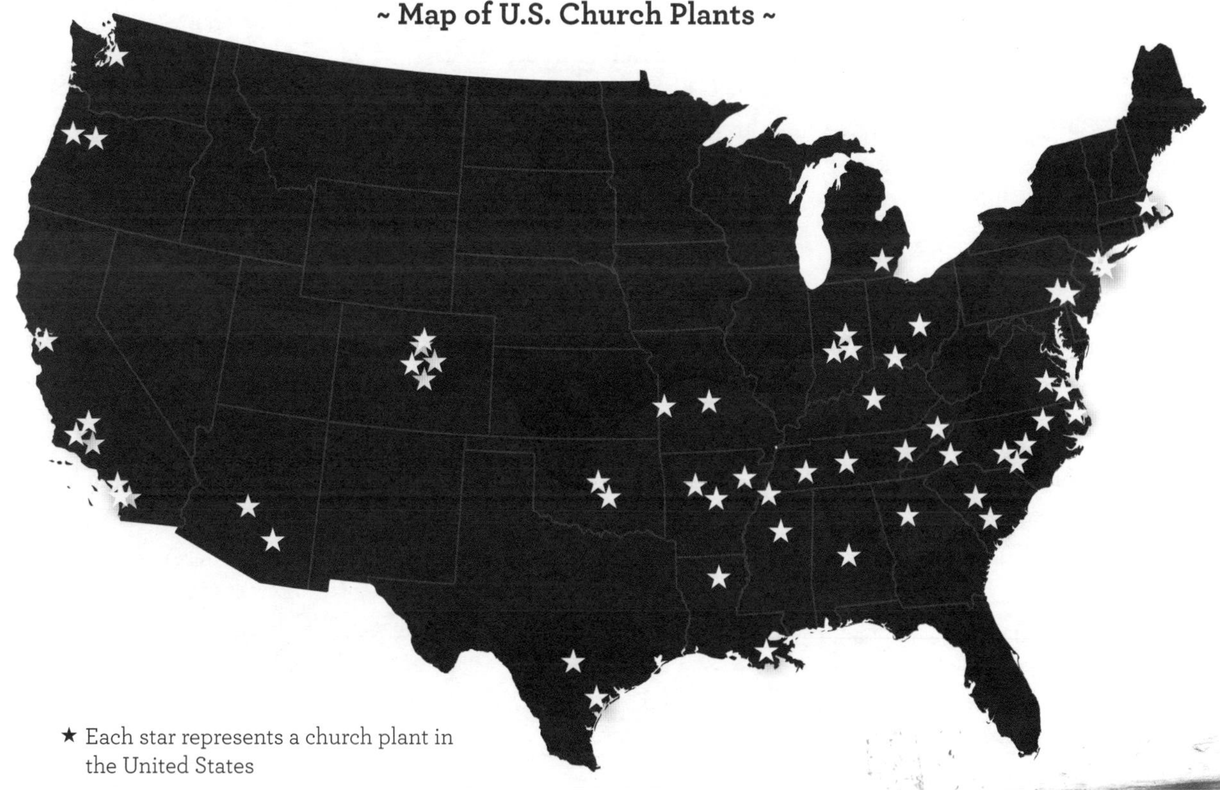

★ Each star represents a church plant in the United States

The **Presenters**

BRYAN CARTER

Bryan Carter taught the original Men's Fraternity curriculum to a group of more than 800 men over a three-year period at Concord Church. Additionally, he has been a frequent speaker at local and international churches, conferences and events.

Bryan is the Senior Pastor of Concord Church in Dallas, Texas.

He is the author of a 28-day devotional book entitled *Great Expectations*. Bryan also contributed to the book *What Two White Men of God Learned from Black Men of God*, co-authored by Dr. Joel Gregory and Dr. Bill Crouch.

A recreational basketball player, Bryan is a fan of the NBA's Dallas Mavericks.

Bryan and his wife Stephanie are the parents of two daughters, Kaitlyn and Kennedy, and one son, Carson.

TIERCE GREEN

Tierce Green teaches the principles of Authentic Manhood to well over a thousand men each week at a gathering called *The Quest*. He has traveled extensively as a speaker at conferences and training events,.

Tierce is the Executive Pastor of Small Groups at Woodlands Church in The Woodlands, Texas.

Tierce has written curriculum for Student Life, The North American Mission Board, and LifeWay. His most recent project is a 12-session series for men called *Fight Club: Some Things Are Worth Fighting For.*

A lifelong Dallas Cowboys fan, Tierce's favorite activities include landscaping, grilling just about anything and hanging out in environments that are conducive to good converation.

He and his wife Dana have one daughter, Anna.

JOHN BRYSON

Seeing firsthand the impact the original Men's Fraternity curriculum had on his own life, John Bryson decided to teach the material himself. In the years since, he has led thousands of men through the basic ideas of biblical manhood.

John is a co-founding teaching pastor of Fellowship Memphis in Memphis, Tennessee.

In 2010, he completed his Docto of Ministry from Gordon-Conwe Theological Seminary. John is also the author of *College Ready*, a curriculum for college student and travels the country consultir and investing in churches, churc planters, and leaders.

A native of Harlan, Kentucky, John played baseball at Asbury College.

He and his wife Beth have 5 children: Brooke, Beck, Bo, Boss, and Blair.

Idols

SESSION **ONE** | Training Guide

Idols Presented by Bryan Carter

I. TEMPTATIONS, TRAPS AND IDOLS[1]

1. We're going to help you get to the root issue, the ____________________ beneath the sin.

II. KEY REALITIES

1. You've got to be willing to pursue "ruthless honesty"[2] in the company of trustworthy men.

   - " All of us live in fear of exposure. We don't want the worst things about us to be known... we posture and wear masks. We establish elaborate facades and hide behind our good deeds. This refusal to be truly known and exposed keeps us stuck in our sin."[3] - Author David White

2. There's no such thing as life apart from________________________and temptation.

   - " For the desires of the flesh are against the Spirit, and the desires of the Spirit are against the flesh, for these are opposed to each other, to keep you from doing the things you want to do." Galatians 5:17 (ESV)

3. Grace. Something given to you apart from anything you've ____________________.

   - " The marker of those who understand the gospel of Jesus Christ is that when they stumble and fall, when they screw up, they run TO God and not FROM Him, because they clearly understand that their acceptance before God is not predicated upon their behavior but on the righteous life of Jesus Christ and His sacrificial death."[4]
- Pastor Matt Chandler

[1] The content of this session, especially as it relates to idolatry, has been influenced by the following works: Timothy Keller, *Counterfeit Gods: The Empty Promises of Money, Sex, and Power, and the Only Hope that Matters* (New York: Riverhead Books, 2009); idem., *Paul's Letter to the Galatians: Leader's Guide* (New York: Redeemer Presbyterian, 2003), 106–113; Darrin Patrick, *"Idol-Shattering" in Church Planter: The Man, The Message, The Mission* (Wheaton: Crossway, 2010), 155–172; David Powlison, *Seeing with New Eyes: Counseling and the Human Condition through the Lens of Scripture* (Philadelphia: P&R Publishing, 2003).

[2] David White, *Sexual Sanity for Men: Re-Creating Your Mind in a Crazy Culture* (Greensboro: New Growth Press, 2012).

[3] Ibid., 199-213.

[4] Matt Chandler with jared Wilson, *The Explicit Gospel* (Wheaton: Crossway, 2012), 211.

4. Authentic Manhood is primarily about heart change.

   - The noble fight against sin and temptation is not just about ______________________ modification.

   - Behavior modification without heart change is dangerous.

III. A FRAMEWORK OF IDOLATRY

1. All wrong behavior ultimately goes back to a ______________________ problem.

   - "Idolatry" is when we allow anything other than God to become the center of our heart's true happiness, contentment, meaning, identity, purpose, or security. It's when we allow something else to become an idol or a "surrogate god" in our life, ruling our thoughts, emotions and behaviors.

   - "Idolatry is always the reason we ever do anything wrong. Why do we ever lie or fail to love or keep promises or live unselfishly?... The specific answer is always that there is something besides Jesus Christ that you feel you must have to be happy, something that is more important to your heart than God... The secret to change is always to identify the IDOLS OF THE HEART."[5] - Pastor Tim Keller

2. A few things to know about idols:

   - An idol can be anything—even a ______________________ thing.

     - An idol is anything that competes with God for your heart's affections.

   - Idolatry is built on a ______________________.

   - Idols come from legitimate desires that are being expressed in inordinate or inappropriate ways.

[5]Tim Keller, *Paul's Letter to the Galatians: Leader's Guide* (New York: Redeemer Presbyterian, 2003), 108.

- For our framework, it is helpful to organize idols into two categories:

    - "Surface" Idols:
        - obvious and easily recognizable
        - related to external behavior

    - "Deep" Idols:
        - core desires that rule our hearts
        - motivating voices behind surface idols

3. Three Deep Idols

- The Deep Idol of CONTROL

    - THE LIE:
      If I can just maintain influence or mastery over this situation... these people... my performance... my schedule... my income or whatever, then I'll be okay, content, strong, and safe.

    - FUNCTIONAL HEAVEN:
      Having certainty or ________________________

    - BIGGEST FEAR:
      Instability or weakness

    - WAYS IT CAN PLAY OUT:

-Relentless pursuit of SECURITY
-Excessive pursuit of POWER

- The Deep Idol of SIGNIFICANCE
  - THE LIE:
    If this person, this social group, the colleagues in my profession, if they find me worthy of attention or love, if they acknowledge my value or greatness, as long as I am not being disgraced before them, then I'll be worthy, important, and acceptable.
  - FUNCTIONAL HEAVEN:
    Receiving affirmation and being made to feel important
  - BIGGEST FEAR:
    Rejection or ______________________________
  - WAYS IT CAN PLAY OUT:
    -Overwhelming need for APPROVAL or LOVE
    -Inordinate desire for RECOGNITION

- The Deep Idol of COMFORT
  - THE LIE:
    If I can just maintain physical ease or relaxation, if life can just be laid back, if I can just keep away from stress or responsibility, if I can just experience some pleasure or enjoyment in the moment, then life will be more fulfilling, easy, fun, or thrilling.
  - FUNCTIONAL HEAVEN:
    ________________________ and ease

- BIGGEST FEAR:
  Boredom or responsibility

- WAYS IT CAN PLAY OUT:
  - -Avoid STRESS and RESPONSIBILITY
  - -Constant COMSUMPTION

DISCUSSION / REFLECTION QUESTIONS

1. Refer to the "FOUR KEY REALITIES" on pages 18- 19. Which one is the most important for you to remember in this season of your life? Why?

2. You heard today that idols often start out as good things and come from legitimate desires but can be turned into a bad thing. When do you think something crosses the line from being a good thing or a legitimate desire into an idol?

3. Use the list of DIAGNOSTIC QUESTIONS on pages 22-23 to begin processing which of the Deep Idols you identify with the most. Control, significance, or comfort? How do you think that Deep Idol is manifesting itself in your life right now?

4. Write down (page 16) and share with your group your one or two STRATEGIC MOVES that you need to make in order to apply what you've learned in this session.

AUTHENTIC MANHOOD

YOUR STRATEGIC MOVE

RESOURCES ON THE FOLLOWING PAGES:

FOUR KEY REALITIES ESSENTIAL TO DEALING WITH TEMPTATION

RUTHLESS H

STRUGGLE &

TEMPTATIO

GRAC

HEART CH

- STOP PRETENDING
- REMOVE THE MASK
- YOU'RE A MESS AND I'M A MESS
- MUST BECOME A WAY OF LIFE

ROKEN MEN LIVING IN A BROKEN WORLD
VE HAVE NATURAL UNHEALTHY DESIRES FOR THINGS IN THIS WORLD
VEN WITH CHRIST, WE HAVE TENSION IN OUR DESIRES
ESIRES OF THE FLESH ARE OPPOSED TO DESIRES OF THE SPIRIT
DOLS DISTRACT US FROM OUR HIGHEST GOOD

- A FREE GIFT
- NOT CONTINGENT ON YOUR PERFORMANCE
- BASED ON THE RIGHTEOUS LIFE OF JESUS CHRIST
- MOTIVATES US TO RUN TO GOD NOT FROM HIM
- JESUS ALREADY PAID YOUR PRICE

- THE NOBLE FIGHT IS NOT ABOUT JUST BEHAVIOR MODIFICATION
- BEHAVIOR MODIFICATION WITHOUT HEART CHANGE IS DANGEROUS
- MERE BEHAVIOR MODIFICATION CAN HIDE DEEPER ISSUES
- THE HEART DRIVES US TOWARDS CERTAIN ACTIONS, ATTITUDES AND BEHAVIOR

GOING DEEP: A FRAMEWO[R]K OF IDOLATRY

SIN
TEMPTATIONS
SURFACE IDOLS
STRUGGLES MANHOOD TRAPS EXTERNAL BEHAVIOR

DEEP IDOLS

CONTROL

SIGNIFICANCE

COMFORT

100' ASL
0' SEA LEVEL
100' BSL
200' BSL
300' BSL
400' BSL
500' BSL

Diagnose YOUR

11 DIAGNOSTIC QUE

Below are 11 questions, adapted from David Powlison's book, *Seeing with New Eyes*, to to give you insights that may help you identify possible idols in your life.

1. What do I worry about most?

2. What, if I failed or lost it, would cause me to feel that I did not even want to live?

3. What do I run to in order to comfort myself when things go bad or get difficult?

4. What do I do to cope? What are my release valves? What do I need to f better?

5. What oftentimes preoccupies me? What do I always daydream abou

An idol is anything that competes with God for your heart's affection.

Pastor Martin Lloyd-Jones has said an idol is usually whatever "rouses and attracts me so easily that I give my time, my attention, my energy and my money to it effortlessly."

ONS

What makes me feel the most self-worth? Of what am I the proudest? For what do I want to be known?

What do I often lead with in conversations?

Early on what do I want to make sure that people know about me?

What prayer, unanswered, would make me seriously think about turning away from God?

What do I really want and expect out of life? What do I think would make me happy?

Whom or what do I trust in for my future?

Sources: 2011 United States Bureau of Labor Statistics study; tmsinteractive.com, "How Many Americans Work More Than 40 a Week?" by Shauna Wright; 2011 Ad Council Fatherhood Survey George Barna, Barna Research Archives: Money, Barna Rese Group, Survey of American Christians; American Express Spending and Saving Tracker by Echo Research

TIME WELL SPENT?

One method to help you discover idols in your life is to closely examine the way you spend your time and money. Devoting less attention to being the man God wants you to be while being obsessed with over -pleasing your boss? Working to perfect your short game at the expense of missing key moments with your kids? Using your financial resources exclusively to build a kingdom for yourself rather than also investing them in a Kingdom that'll last forever? Overwhelmed by economic challenges and working as hard as you can to keep up with the Jones?

Let's take a look at what the statistics say about men and the ways they allocate some of their personal resources:

11 Number, in millions, of workers who spend more than 59 hours a week in the workplace; again, the highest percentage worldwide.

---

33 Percent of Christians who say it's impossible for them to get ahead in life because of the financial debt they've incurred.

5.55 Number of hours a day, on average, men devote to leisure activities.

1,084 Number of hours per year, on average, men watch television.

---

142 Number of hours per year, on average, men exercise or pursue recreational activities.

---

86 Percentage of men who say they spend more time with their children than their father did with them.

3-5 Percent of people who give to their church, who actually follow the biblical model of tithing; that is, giving ten percent of one's income.

SCRIPTURE REFERENCES

Psalm 16:11 (ESV) "You make known to me the path of life; in your presence there is fullness of joy; at your right hand are pleasures forevermore."

Proverbs 19:21 (ESV) "Many are the plans in the mind of a man, but it is the purpose of the Lord that will stand."

Mark 21:22 (ESV) "For from within, out of the heart of man, come evil thoughts, sexual immorality, theft, murder, adultery, coveting, wickedness, deceit, sensuality, envy, slander, pride, foolishness."

Galatians 1:10 (ESV) "For am I now seeking the approval of man, or of God? Or am I trying to please man? If I were still trying to please man, I would not be a servant of Christ."

Galatians 5:17 (ESV) "The desires of the flesh are against the Spirit, and the desires of the Spirit are against the flesh, for these are opposed to each other, to keep you from doing the things you want to do."

Colossians 3:23-24 (ESV) "Whatever you do, work heartily, as for the Lord and not for men, knowing that from the Lord you will receive the inheritance as your reward."

SUPPORTING RESOURCES

Keller, Timothy. ***Counterfeit Gods: The Empty Promises of Money, Sex, and Power, and the Only Hope that Matters.*** **Riverhead, 2009.** Pastor and *New York Times* Bestselling Author, Tim Keller, provides a very succint and highly readable overview of idolatry and how to fight against it.

Powlison, David. ***"Idols of the Heart and 'Vanity Fair'"*** **The Journal of Biblical Counseling 13 (1995): 35-50 .** Online: https://www.ccef.org/idols-heart-andvanity-fair. David Powlison provides an in-depth look at idolatry from a counselor's perspective.

**The content in the resources above does not necessarily reflect the opinion of Authentic Manhood. Readers should utilize these resources but form their own opinions.*

Empty Promises

SESSION **TWO** | Training Guide

Empty Promises Presented by John Bryson

I. INTRODUCTION AND REVIEW

1. Manhood traps and sin have a deeper source within us, rather than simply being surface actions and external decisions that we make.

2. Life-change and true transformation will not happen until we can learn to identify and deal with the ________________________ of our sin.

3. The Three Deep Idols:

4. "For my people have committed two evils: they have forsaken me, the fountain of living waters, and hewed out cisterns for themselves, broken cisterns that can hold no water." Jeremiah 2:13 (ESV)

5. Idols lure us away from the __________________ God has for us in His grace.

6. This lesson will look at the struggle with idolatry in the lives of three central figures from the Bible:

   - Adam
   - King Solomon
   - The Apostle Paul

II. ADAM: IDOLS IN PARADISE

1. Adam bought into the orginial lie, which is the foundational lie for all idols: that we must go around God and away from God, rather than to God, to meet our deepest needs.

Satan Tempting Adam

The Lie	The Deep Idol
Genesis 3:5 "You'll be like God"	Satan appealing to the idols of Control and Significance
Genesis 3:6 "The Fruit is a Delight"	Satan appealing to the idol of Comfort

2. The lie offered by the deep idols: there's a ________________________ way than what God has provided.

III. KING SOLOMON: CHASING IDOL FANTASIES

- Ecclesiastes documents Solomon's all-out pursuit of happiness in the "broken cisterns that do not hold water."

3. Wisdom and Knowledge

- Solomon chased wisdom and knowledge. "And I applied my heart to seek and to search out by wisdom all that is done under heaven." Ecclesiastes 1:13

- Solomon concluded: "I have acquired great wisdom, surpassing all who were over Jerusalem before me, and my heart has had great experience of wisdom and knowledge. And I applied my heart to know widsom and to know madness and folly.

I perceived that this also is but a striving after the wind." Ecclesiastes 1:16-17 (ESV)

4. Pleasure

- Solomon said, "I said in my heart, 'Come now, I will test you with ____________________; enjoy yourself.'" Ecclesiastes 2:1 (ESV)

- All he found was vanity.

5. Excessive Alcohol[1]

- Solomon found that drunkenness was not a solution for happiness.

6. Accomplishments

- Solomon tried to put his hope and identity in this ____________________ idol.

7. Wealth

- "He who loves money will not be satisfied with money, nor he who loves wealth, with his income; this also is vanity." Ecclesiastes 5:10 (ESV)

8. Sex

- Even with 1,000 women at his disposal, Solomon found it all vanity.

9. Work

- Solomon found that work makes for a terrible ____________________- another broken cistern.

[1]As mentioned in the session, according to one recent study, 43% of men engaged in binge drinking over the past year—that's defined as at least 5 drinks or more within 2 hours. Online: Http://www.niaaa.nih.gov/alcohol-health/overview-alcohol-comsumption/drinking-statistcs.

IV. PAUL: THE IDOL OF SELF-RIGHTEOUSNESS

- Paul describes his impressive, self-righteous résumé (which in his day, would have placed him in the "who's - who" of the religious elite): "If anyone else thinks he has reason for confidence in the flesh, I have more: circumcised on the eighth day, of the people of Israel, of the tribe of Benjamin, a Hebrew of Hebrews; as to the law, a Pharisee; as to zeal, a persecutor of the church; as to righteousness under the law, blameless." Philippians 3:4-6 (ESV)

- Paul concludes later that:"But whatever gain I had, I counted it as loss for the sake of Christ. Indeed, I count everything as loss because of the surpassing worth of knowing Christ Jesus my Lord. For His sake I have suffered the loss of all things and count them as rubbish, in order that I may gain Christ." Philippians 3:7-8 (ESV)

- Your Deep Idols of CONTROL and SIGNIFICANCE can manifest themselves in religious discipline, ______________________, or more church.

V. CONCLUSION

1. It's helpful to see that as a man, you are not __________________. All of us struggle with this stuff.

2. All good things can become sinful things if we make them the main things.

3. Solomon's conclusion: "Enjoy life, don't ______________________ life."

DISCUSSION / REFLECTION QUESTIONS

1. Reflect on Solomon's story. Is there any part of you that would like to try to find fulfillment in unlimited money, pleasure, excessive alcohol, power, sex, success, achievements, etc? If you did, do you think you would come to the same conclusion as Solomon? That it's all vanity, like chasing after the wind?

2. Share something that can be an idol in your life and the empty promise that you're tempted to believe.

3. Check out the insights of the 3 men on pages 34-35 who "had it all." What do they reveal to you?

4. Are you ever tempted toward the idol of self-righteousness as the apostle Paul was at one time in his life? What can that look like in your life?

5. Write down (on page 33) and share with your group your one or two STRATEGIC MOVES that you need to make in order to apply what you've learned in this session.

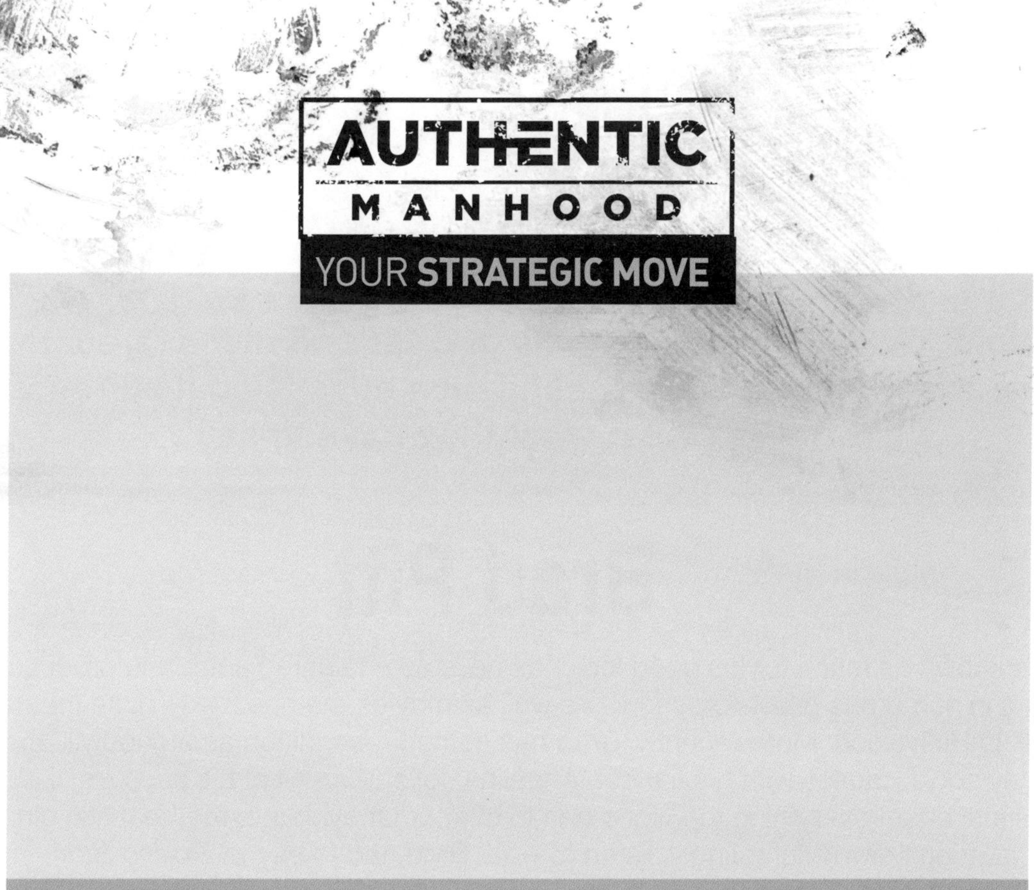

RESOURCES ON THE FOLLOWING PAGES:

- "Having It All" (p. 34-35)
- Article: *More Broken Cisterns* (p. 36-39)
- **THE RED ZONE**: The Truth About Idols (p. 40-41)

"HAVING IT ALL"

Solomon had all the world has to offer and discovered it was no[t] enough. These 3 successful men have "had it all" as well. Let's hear what they have to say…

Brad Pitt

Brad is known as much for his good looks as he is as a talented actor and producer. Starring in numerous television shows as well as movies, he has made quite the name for himself in Hollywood. More recently, Brad has gained recognition as a goodwill ambassado[r] for many social causes with his fiancée Angelina Jolie. With all of his success, it appears he has just about everything the world has to offer...money, fame, the beautiful girl, great looks, stardom, etc. Interestingly, listen to what Brad had to say to *Rolling Stone* magazine near the peak of his career:

"Hey, man, I don't have those answers yet. The emphasis now is on success and personal gain. I'm sitting in it, and I'm telling you, that's not it. I'm the guy who's got everything. I know. But I'm telling you, once you've got everything, then you're just left with yourself. I've said it before and I'll say it again: **it doesn't help you sleep any better, and you don't wake up any better because of it."**

Tom Brady

›m is one of the most successful quarterbacks in NFL history. He is a certain future all-of-Famer and has won numerous regular season and Super Bowl MVP honors. an interview with "60 Minutes," not long after signing a $60 million contract, he shared ı interesting perspective on his amazing success:

Vhy do I have three Super Bowl rings and still think there's something greater out there r me? I mean, maybe a lot of people would say, 'Hey man, this is what is.' I reached my ›al, my dream, my life. Me, I think, **'God, it's got to be more than this.'"**

Wayne Huizenga, Jr

ɾne is the President of Huizenga Holdings, Inc., a diversified company that owns the Miami ›hins and Dolphins Stadium as well as investments in resorts and real estate. The Huizengas one of the most successful business families in modern American history. In an interview with n Second," he reaches a conclusion that sounds a lot like Solomon's:

ore Christ, I was self-focused. I was going to do what I wanted to please me, no matter t that meant. That was my life. I had wealth, a nice sports fishing yacht, lived in a big home, an incredible amount of disposable income, owned three sports teams, drank in excess, t to clubs that you didn't tell your mom about, demanded an audience, said whatever came y mind whether it was to you or your wife…self-focused, to do what I wanted to please me. ife was this incredible banquet of all the things that the world had to offer, **but just never ing full, never being satisfied, never being able to push away and say that's enough.'"**

1. Chris Heath, "The Unbearable Bradness of Being (Cover Story)," *Rolling Stone* no. 824:66, 1999. *Academic Search Premier*, EBSCOhost (accessed May 9, 2013).
2. Daniel Schorn, "Tom Brady: The Winner," CBS *60 Minutes*, December 20, 2007.
3. Wayne Huizenga, Jr., "I Am Second," *http://www.iamsecond.com/seconds/wayne-huizenga*

MORE BROKEN CISTERNS

BIBLICAL FIGURES AND THEIR IDOLS

SAMSON

BY JOHN BRYSON

Samson's life serves as a warning for every man in his wake. His story is the classic biography of a man who put his hope and trust in himself and in his own gifts and talents. You are left thinking at the end of his life, which incidently ends on a suicide mission, "What could Samson's story have been?"

Samson was born into almost every advantage possible. He was chosen by God to be born to two loving parents who were worshippers of God and who loved their son. He was set apart by God in the womb and God chose Samson to be a deliverer of his people, the Israelites.

The story quickly takes a dark turn as idols of lust and sex surface early. Lust and illicit sex are a theme throughout Samson's life. Anger, rage, and power are lifelong companions as well.

Samson's whole biography is found in the book of Judges. In chapter 14, he has a lustful encounter with a woman "who looked good to him." Despite warnings by God and his parents, Samson pursues this woman and it ends in disaster. We see him also solicit a prostitute a couple of chapters later in Judges 16. The third woman in Samson's life, Delilah, was a deceitful enemy of Samson who ultimately betrayed him. Samson's idols of lust and sex over-promised and under-delivered. They destroyed him.

Let Samson be a warning to us all. God's gifts and talents entrusted to each of us as men can be used for God's glory, or our own pursuit of idols. The former leads to the abundant life, the latter leads to death.

PETER

BY JOHN BRYSON

We first meet Peter in the Bible as a fisherman who has a radical, life-altering encounter with Jesus. He leaves fishing for fish to learn how to become a fisher of men. He becomes on of Jesus' disciples and follow him for three years. In those three years, God did more in Peter than He did through Peter. There was some idol surgery that needed to be done.

I love Peter, probably because I can personally relate to Him. Peter is aggressive, opinionated, and very "ready, fire, aim." So am I! Peter has a foot-shaped mouth! So do I!

Among the idols we see in Peter's life are idols of control, comfort, and significance. Control rears its head in a famous scene in a garden when Peter is with Jesus and the authorities are closing in on them. Peter takes the moment into his own hands and takes a sword and, probably swinging for his head, clips off an ear of a Centurion guard. Later, we see Peter bow at the idol of comfort by denying Christ three times, fearful of what would happen to him if he was associated with Jesus. Finally, w see Jesus tenderly deal with Peter's significance idol by forgivin Peter and embracing him after his denial. In the midst of Peter' shame, guilt, and feelings of insignificance, Jesus breathes into Peter grace, forgiveness, and life.

DAVID

BY BRYAN CARTER

David is known as a man after God's own heart. Historically, he is seen as one of th greatest figures in Scripture.

David grew up in a family of insecurity whe little was expected of him. Yet, even through these challenges, he developed a strong fait in God. He experienced the early victory ove Goliath that gave him great prominence, as well as the anointing of God on life as the next king.

However, even with great success, none of us are exempt from a stuggle with idols of our heart. David's idol was sex. 2 Samuel 11 captures the pin of this idol in his life. In this chapter, we watch David allow the idol of sex t consume his life. David no longer is functioning as the man of faith we are familiar with but instead has fully submitted to this idol. David takes anoth man's wife to have sex with her, attempts to cover it up, has her husband murdered, marries her and then believes that he has gotten away with it. I is only when the prophet, Nathan, confronts him that he begins the path t overcoming his idol.

David fought his idol by restoring his relationship with God. Psalm 51 is expression of a man reacting to a desire to remove the idols of his heart ar replace them with a right relationship with God. In Psalm 51:10, David wri "Create in me a clean heart, O God, and renew a right spirit within me." Da models for us that, as men, we must face our idols head on. Denial only le to greater damage. Battling our idols is a heart issue and we must be willir trust God fully to renew us and give us a heart that fully pursues Him.

Jonah's life is wrapped around one assignment that God gave him, "To go to inevah and preach against the wickedness in ıe city." However, Jonah refuses to go and runs ıe opposite direction. He becomes a "Runaway rophet" who is determined to have matters his ay. His rationale for this is that he believed that inevah did not deserve the grace of God in their lives. He runs away until od sends a storm and a fish to get his attention and it is only after three ays in the belly of a fish that he relents to commit to God's assignment.

The idol of Jonah's life was control. Jonah had to be in control at all times, ven when it came to his relationship with God. He simply believed that he ıew best and that his way was ultimately the best for all. The idol of control work in the life of Jonah produced stubbornness, arrogance, and self-estructive habits. His heart was wrapped around himself and he became tally disconnected from God.

Yet, while Jonah was in the belly of the fish, he began to come to his enses and states in Jonah 2:8-9, "Those who pay to regard to vain idols rsake their hope of steadfast love. But I with the voice of thanksgiving will crifice to you; what I have vowed I will pay. Salvation belongs to the LORD!"

He wages war against his idol by learning that only in submitting to God oes he find true peace. Although Jonah battles with this idol throughout his e, he learns that God ultimately is in control and that his best position in e is to be fully submitted and surrendered to Him.

Control freak? Probably not, but it is safe to say that the Apostle Paul was driven. And men who are driven can easily fall into traps rooted in the deep idol of control, especially the workaholism trap and the power trap.

Before his conversion, he was known as Saul of Tarsus. He was one of the religious elite—a arisee—and Pharisees defined themselves by their religious efforts, which ey believed controlled their favor with God.

Saul fell into the power trap and became a relentless persecutor of the urch. The power trap is when you want other people to submit to you, perience you as a man of consequence, and fear you. But God can ange anyone.

When Saul encountered the resurrected Christ on the Damascus Road, submitted to the truth of Jesus, converted to Christianity and was ıamed Paul. The clarity in his explanation of the gospel gave the early urches a solid foundation and a healthy framework.

magine all those "aha!" moments as Paul discovered how the Scriptures thought he had mastered actually exposed mankind's epic fail and how ey were pointing us to God's provision of grace in Jesus. He captured this ofound truth in one clear and succinct statement: "For by grace you have en saved through faith. And this is not your own doing; it is the gift of God, a result of works, so that no one may boast."[1]

he revelation of God's grace did not turn Paul into a slacker. He still rked hard—three long missionary journeys throughout the Roman Empire nting churches, preaching the gospel, and encouraging new believers— it was from the right position in Christ and for the right purpose. "I can all things through Christ who strengthens me"[2] fueled his passion. Paul laced the self-effort lie of control with the truth of God's grace in Jesus.

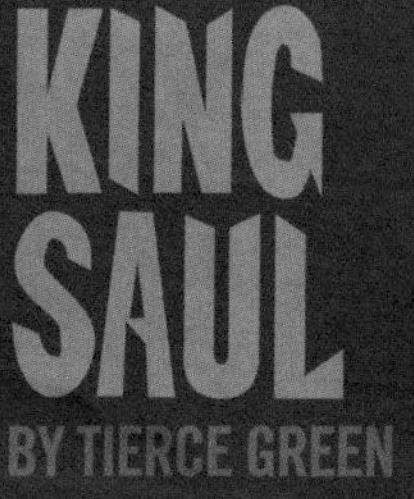

When the Prophet Samuel revealed to Saul that he was God's choice to be Israel's first king, Saul immediately expressed feelings of insignificance. He pointed out that he was "from the smallest tribe of Israel," and that his clan was "the least of all the clans."[3] Saul saw himself as small in his own eyes.[4]

Samuel gave him a stunning affirmation: "Do you see the man the Lord has chosen? There is no one like him among all the people."[5] A man should be humbled by that and build on God's favor. But Saul found his significance in the opinions of others. That's the approval trap, which is rooted in the deep idol of significance.

Early in his reign, King Saul made a fatal mistake. He failed to completely destroy the Amalekites and all their possessions, as God had commanded. After trying to justify his actions, he finally admits that he violated God's command. He said, "I feared the people and obeyed their voice."[6]

The Lord withdrew his favor from Saul and had Samuel anoint David as king.[7] The approval of the people was off the charts for David and just so-so for Saul: "Saul has slain his thousands, and David his tens of thousands!"[8]

Saul went into a jealous rage and plotted to kill David. He had lost God's favor and his jealousy drove him to madness. Surrounded by the Philistines on Mount Gilboa, he lost his sons. In the end, King Saul fell on his sword and lost his life.

Tragically, Saul missed out on what God designed him to experience. He allowed the deep idol of significance to destroy his life and his legacy.

[1] Ephesians 2:8-9 (ESV)
[2] Philippians 4:13 (NKJV)
[3] 1 Samuel 9:21 (NIV)
[4] "And Samuel said, 'Though you are little in your own eyes, are you not the head of the tribes of Israel? The Lord anointed you king over Israel.'" 1 Samuel 15:17 (ESV)
[5] 1 Samuel 10:24 (NIV)
[6] 1 Samuel 15:24 (ESV)
[7] "You have rejected the word of the Lord, and the Lord has rejected you as king over Israel!" 1 Samuel 15:26 (NIV)
[8] 1 Samuel 18:7, (NIV)

The TRUTH a bou

"My people have committed two evils: They have forsaken me, the fountain of living waters, and hewed out cisterns for themselves, broken cisterns that can hold no water."
- Jeremiah 2:13 -

dols

- Idols are like broken cisterns that don't hold water. They cannot satisfy us.
- Idols cannot satisfy the longings of our soul.
- Idols always over-promise and under-deliver.
- Idols lure us away from the best God has for us.
- Idols are full of lies.
- Idols are God-substitutes.
- Idols are good things that we make the main thing and thus become sinful things.
- Idols are anything we look to, other than God, for our ultimate meaning, validation, and purpose.

SCRIPTURE REFERENCES

Jeremiah 2:13 (ESV) " My people have committed two evils: they have forsaken me, the fountain of living waters, and hewed out cisterns for themselves, broken cisterns that can hold no water. "

Philippians 3:4-8 (ESV) " If anyone else thinks he has reason for confidence in the flesh, I have more: circumcised on the eighth day, of the people of Israel, of the tribe of Benjamin, a Hebrew of Hebrews; as to the law, a Pharisee; as to zeal, a persecutor of the church; as to righteousness under the law, blameless. But whatever gain I had, I counted as loss for the sake of Christ. Indeed, I count everything as loss because of the surpassing worth of knowing Christ Jesus my Lord. For his sake I have suffered the loss of all things and count them as rubbish, in order that I may gain Christ."

SUPPORTING RESOURCES

Nelson, Tommy. *A Life Well Lived: A Study of the Book of Ecclesiates.* Broadman and Holman, 2005. This book provides an overview of Solomon's pursuit for meaning and purpose, written by one of the best modern expositors of Ecclesiastes.

Ryken, Philip Graham. *Ecclesiastes: Why Everything Matters.* Crossway, 2010. Phillip Ryken, President of Wheaton College, provides a chapter-by chapter analysis of Ecclesiastes.

**The content in the resources above does not necessarily reflect that opinion of Authentic Manhood. Readers should utilize these resources but form their own opinions.*

Battle Plan

SESSION THREE | Training Guide

Battle Plan Presented by Tierce Green

I. INTRODUCTION

1. Temptations and ____________________ are issues for ALL of us, and this has devastated men throughout history.

2. God is for us, not against us. John 10:10 says that Jesus came so that we could have life.

3. It's not that your desires are too STRONG and need to be dialed back; actually they're too WEAK and need to be ____________________.

4. "If there lurks in most modern minds the notion that to desire our own good and earnestly to hope for the enjoyment of it is a bad thing, I submit that this notion ... is no part of the Christian faith. Indeed, if we consider the unblushing promises of reward and the staggering nature of the rewards promised in the Gospels, it would seem that our Lord finds our desires, not too strong, but too weak. We are half-hearted creatures, fooling around with drink and sex and ambition when infinte joy is offered to us, like an ignorant child who wants to go on making mud pies in a slum because he cannot imagine what is meant by the offer of a holiday at the sea. We are far to easily pleased."[1]
 -C.S. Lewis

5. The problem isn't desire. The problem is ____________________ desire.

II. NOBLE PATHWAYS

1. God's NOBLE pathways are ultimately more lasting and more fulfilling than ANY alternative.[2]

2. You can't just REMOVE an idol or behavior from your life. You have to ____________________ it with something else, something more satisfying and fulfilling.

[1] C.S.Lewis , *The Weight of Glory* (New York: Harper Collins, 1949), 26.
[2] In regard to the noble pathway of giving, Tierce mentioned in the session that some recent research supports Jesus' promise that we'd be far "happier than getting"(Acts 20:35, The Message). For an overview of this research see Elizabeth Dunn and Michael Norton, "Don't Indulge. Be Happy," *The New York Times*, July 7, 2012. Online: *http://www.nytimes,com/2012/07/08/opinion/sunday/dont-indulge-be-happy.html.*

3. God has created NOBLE pathways to meet our God-given desires.

III. ULYSSES AND JASON ILLUSTRATION

1. The Ulysses and Jason story illustrated the two different strategies we can adopt when it comes to dealing with temptation and idols.

- Ulysses
  - We can try to hold ourselves back
  - Life becomes a bunch of "don'ts" and we make God the fun-killer

- Jason
  - Drown out temptation by being captivated by God

IV. OUR "BATTLE PLAN"

1. ADMIT the struggle
2. IDENTIFY the lie
3. REPLACE with the truth

1. ADMIT the struggle

- The first step is always to own up to the fact that an external issue is causing problems and has become a surface __________________ in your life.

- It's imperative that you be ruthlessly honest about your struggles with one or more trustworthy men. James 5:16 tells us to confess our sins to one another.

- We can remove the mask and begin moving toward God's ______________________.

2. IDENTIFY the Lie

- All three of the Deep Idols promise us ________________________________, but their promises never deliver.

To help identify the lies you're believing, see the Diagnostic Questions from Session 1 - "Idols " (page 22-23).

3. REPLACE with the truth

- You must believe the truth that Jesus has already paid the price for all of your sins.

- God's ______________________ is the most powerful thing in the universe.

- We __________________________ the idol lies we have believed in the past with the truth and power of GRACE offered in Christ and in the truth of God's Word.

- True life-change begins with the renewing of our minds (Romans 12:2).

V. JESUS' EXAMPLE

1. Just like Adam in the Garden of Eden, Jesus was tempted by the great liar himself, Satan.

- Temptation #1 - The Deep Idol of _____________________________
    - Satan: "If you are the Son of God, command these stones to become loaves of bread." Matthew 4:3 (ESV)
    - Jesus' response: "It is written, 'Man shall not live by bread alone, but by every word that comes from the mouth of God.'" Matthew 4:4 (ESV) (Jesus Quoting from the Old Testament, Deuteronomy 8:3)

- Temptation #2 - The Deep Idol of _______________________________

- Satan: "If you are the Son of God, throw yourself down, for it is written, 'He will command His angels concerning you,' and 'on their hands they will bear you up, lest you strike your foot against a stone.'" -Matthew 4:6 (ESV)

- Jesus' response: "It is written, 'You shall not put the Lord your God to the test.'" Matthew 4:7 (ESV) (Jesus quoting from the Old Testament, Deuteronomy 6:16)

- Temptation #3 - The Deep Idol of ________________________

  - Satan: "All these I will give you [all the kingdoms of the world], if you will fall down and worship me." Matthew 4:9 (ESV)

  - Jesus' response: "Be gone, Satan! For it is written, 'You shall worship the Lord your God and Him only shall you serve.'" Matthew 4:10 (ESV) (Jesus quoting from the Old Testament, Deuteronomy 6:13)

See the "War in the Wilderness" Red Zone on page 60

2. Jesus turned to the more satisfying________________________ to repel the false lies.

3. "Our chief enemy is the lie that says sin will make our future happier. Our chief weapon is the truth that says God will make our future happier... When my thirst for joy and meaning and passion are satisfied by the presence and promises of Christ, the power of sin is broken. We do not yield to the offer of sandwich meat when we can smell the steak sizzling on the grill."[3] - Pastor John Piper

VI. EXAMPLES OF REPLACING IDOLS

1. Idol of CONTROL

- The Lie: Happiness comes when ____________________ running the show.

- The Truth: "Trust God and don't be anxious about your life, what you will eat or

[3]John Piper, *Future Grace* (Colorado Springs: Maltnomah Press, 1995), 335-336. In its orginal context, the first sentence of this quote actually occurs subsequently to the second two sentences.

what you will drink, nor about your body, what you will put on... But seek first the kingdom of God and His righteousness, and all of these things will be added unto you." Matthew 6:31-33 (ESV)

2. Idol of COMFORT

- The Lie: Happiness comes when life is ______________________ or when I'm consuming.

- The Truth: Jesus teaches us by example that true happiness comes not in immediate gratification but in self-sacrifice for the benefit of others (Hebrews 12:2).

VII. CONCLUSION

1. God is ________________ , not AGAINST our true happiness.

2. You now have a biblical process, a "Battle Plan," to fight fire with fire.

   i. ADMIT the Struggle

   ii. IDENTIFY the lie

   iii. ___________________with the truth

DISCUSSION / REFLECTION QUESTIONS

1. Do you agree with the C.S. Lewis comment that "our Lord finds our desires not too strong, but too weak?" What do you think Lewis means when he says that "we are far too easily pleased?"

2. Are you approaching life more like Ulysses (trying to restrain yourself from doing certain things), or more like Jason (focused on chasing something better)? Do you believe that God's "noble pathways" are ultimately more lasting and more satisfying than any alternative? In what area of your life are you struggling to believe this?

3. Share an issue in your life where you need to apply the "Battle Plan." Describe how you could apply each of the three steps to that issue (see page 52-53).

4. Look over the list of verses listed on pages 56-59 to help assist you in applying the "Battle Plan" ... to help you "renew your mind and replace your idols" with God's truth. Share with your group verses that you think could be the most helpful for you. You may want to make a note to memorize them as part of your Strategic Move.

AUTHENTIC MANHOOD

YOUR STRATEGIC MOVE

RESOURCES ON THE FOLLOWING PAGES:

- The Battle Plan (p. 52-53)
- Renewing Your Mind (p. 54-59)
- **THE RED ZONE**: War in The Wilderness (p. 60-61)

XXXXXXXXXXXXXXXX

Battle PLAN

Admit → Identify → Replace

#1 **Admit** THE STRUGGLE

+ Admit your struggle to yourself and to God. Own up that there is an external issue causing problems and has become an idol in your life.
+ Get an accurate picture of where you REALLY are and what you are REALLY struggling with.
+ Be ruthlessly honest about your struggles with one or more trustworthy men.
+ Avoid the 97% rule. Do not hold back the worst, and potentially most important, details of your struggle.
+ Remove your mask with trustworthy teammates and begin moving toward God's grace.

#2 **Identify** THE LIE

+ Go below the surface and identify the lie that is seducing you, the lie that you are believing at the core of your heart.
+ Remember that all idols over-promise and under-deliver. How is this idol duping you? What is it promising?
+ It helps to work through the diagnostic questions on pages 22-23. They will help you connect your behaviors with the real issues of your heart.

#3 **Replace** WITH THE TRUTH

+ Replace your idols with something that is better, something reliable that comes through… with (1) the truth of grace and forgiveness in Jesus and (2) the more satisfying promises of scripture.
+ Believe with all of your heart in the grace of Jesus, that His gift of salvation makes us come alive in Him.
+ Totally embrace the reality that God's grace is the most powerful thing in the universe.
+ Follow Jesus' example in the wilderness (Matthew 4) by replacing the lies that you are believing with the truth offered in God's Word.
+ Transformation (i.e., true life-change, replacing your idols) begins with the renewing of your mind, by filling your mind with the truth of God's Word.

TRANSFORMATION *begins with* *the* RENEWING *of* YOUR MIND

ROMANS 1

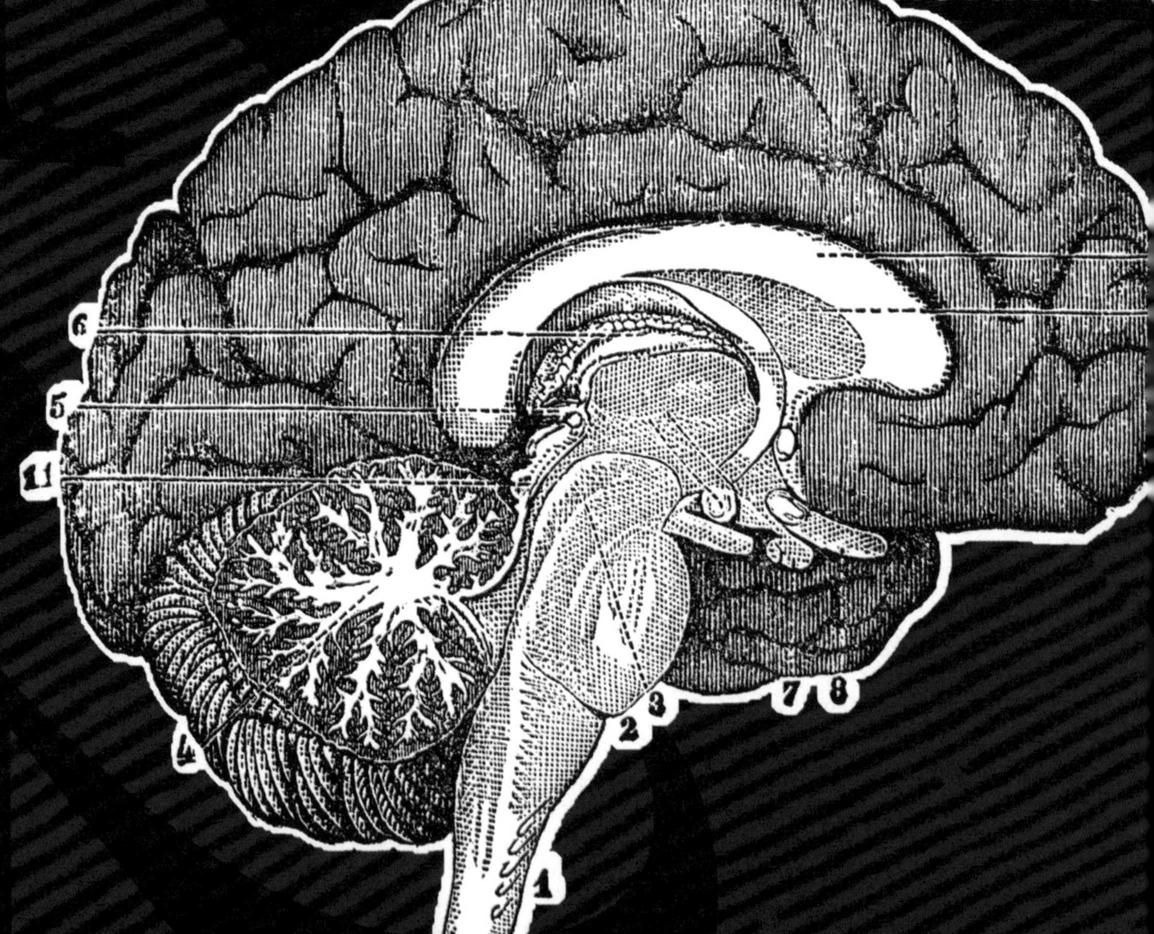

YOUR BEHAVIOR

MAPS OUT A SMALL "ROAD" IN YOUR BRAIN THAT CREATES A BASIC PATHWAY FOR YOUR THOUGHTS.

AS YOU REPEAT A PARTICULAR BEHAVIOR,

YOUR BRAIN BUILDS A BIGGER "HIGHWAY" THAT ALLOWS FOR AN INCREASED (((VOLUME))) AND FREQUENCY OF THOUGHTS TO MOVE ABOUT.

THIS RESULTS IN YOUR **DAY-TO-DAY ACTIONS.**

IN ORDER TO CHANGE YOUR BEHAVIOR, YOU MUST REPROGRAM YOUR BRAIN.

YOU HAVE TO DECONSTRUCT AN EXISTING HIGHWAY AND REPLACE IT WITH A NEW ONE. THIS IS A PROCESS THAT TAKES TIME.

THE BIBLE TEACHES US TO BE TRANSFORMED BY THE **RENEWING OF OUR MIND** THROUGH THE POWER OF GOD'S WORD.

IN TIME, THE RESULT IS THE FORMATION OF AN ENTIRELY NEW NEUROLOGICAL ROADMAP.

LEADING YOU TO **FREEDOM FROM THE PAST** AND TO **THE BETTER LIFE YOU WERE MEANT TO LIVE.**

RENEW YOUR MIND *through the* POWER *of* GOD'S WORD

I. BATTLE PLAN

A. ADMIT THE STRUGGLE

JAMES 5:16 Therefore, confess your sins to one another an
pray for one another, that you may be healed.

PROVERBS 28:13 Whoever conceals his transgressions will not prosper, but he who confesses and forsakes them will obtain mercy.

LUKE 15:7 [Jesus speaking] Just so, I tell you, there will be more joy in heaven over one sinner who repents than over ninety-nine righteous persons who need no repentance.

ROMANS 3:23 For all have sinned and fall short of the glor
of God.

2 CORINTHIANS 7:10 For godly grief produces a repentance that leads to salvation without regret, whereas worldly grief produces death.

GALATIANS 5:17 For the desires of the flesh are against th
Spirit, and the desires of the Spirit are against the flesh, fo
these are opposed to each other, to keep you from doing the things you want to do.

EPHESIANS 4:25 Therefore, having put away falsehood, le
each one of you speak the truth with his neighbor, for we are members of one another.

1 JOHN 1:8–9 [8]If we say we have no sin, we deceive ourselves, and the truth is not in us. [9]If we confess our sins
he is faithful and just to forgive us our sins and to cleanse us from all unrighteousness.

B. IDENTIFY THE LIE

DEUTERONOMY 11:16 Take care lest your heart be deceived, and you turn aside and serve other gods and worship them.

PROVERBS 4:23 Keep your heart with all vigilance, for from it flow the springs of life.

PROVERBS 20:4 The purpose in a man's heart is like deep water, but a man of understanding will draw it out.

LAMENTATIONS 3:40 Let us test and examine our ways, and return to the Lord!

ECCLESIASTES 2:11 Yet when I surveyed all that my hands had done and what I had toiled to achieve, everything was meaningless, a chasing after the wind; nothing was gained under the sun.

JOHN 8:12 [Jesus speaking] I am the light of the world. Whoever follows me will not walk in darkness, but will have the light of life.

EPHESIANS 4:22 Put off your old self, which belongs to your former manner of life and is corrupt through deceitful desires.

EPHESIANS 5:11, 13 [11]Take no part in the unfruitful works of darkness, but instead expose them. . . . [13]when anything is exposed by the light, it becomes visible.

C. REPLACE WITH THE TRUTH

ROMANS 12:2 Do not be conformed to this world, but be transformed by the renewal of your mind, that by testing you may discern what is the will of God, what is good and acceptable and perfect.

DEUTERONOMY 8:4 Man does not live by bread alone, but man lives by every word that comes from the mouth of the Lord.

PSALM 1:1-3 [1]Blessed is the man . . . [2][whose] delight is in the Law of the Lord, and on his law he meditates day and night. He is like a tree planted by streams of water that yields its fruit in its season, and its leaf does not wither.

PSALM 18:30 God—his way is perfect; the word of the Lord proves true; he is a shield for all those who take refuge in him.

PSALM 119:9-11 [9]How can a young man keep his way pure? By guarding it according to your word. [10]With my whole heart I seek you; let me not wander from your commandments! [11]I have stored up your word in my heart, that I might not sin against you.

PSALM 119:105 Your word is a lamp to my feet and a light to my path.

PROVERBS 7:1-3 [1]My son, keep my words and treasure up my commandments with you; keep my commandments and live; [2]keep my teaching as the apple of your eye; [3]bind them on your fingers; write them on the tablet of your heart.

JOHN 8:31-32 [31]"If you abide in my word, you are truly my disciples, [32]and you will know the truth, and the truth will set you free."

ROMANS 8:5-6 [5]For those who live according to the flesh set their minds on the things of the flesh, but those who live according to the Spirit set their minds on the things of the Spirit. [6]For to set the mind on the flesh is death, but to set the mind on the Spirit is life and peace.

1 CORINTHIANS 14:20 Brothers, do not be children in your thinking. Be infants in evil, but in your thinking be mature.

2 CORINTHIANS 4:16-18 [16]So we do not lose heart. Though our outer self is wasting away, our inner self is being renewed day by day. [17]For this light momentary affliction is preparing for us an eternal weight of glory beyond all comparison, [18]as we look not to the things that are seen but to the things that are unseen. For the things that are seen are transient, but the things that are unseen are eternal.

2 CORINTHIANS 10:4-5 [4]For the weapons of our warfare are not of the flesh but have divine power to destroy strongholds. [5]We destroy arguments and every lofty opinion raised against the knowledge of God, and take every thought captive to obey Christ.

EPHESIANS 4:23-24 [23]Be renewed in the spirit of your minds, [24]and . . . put on the new self, created after the likeness of God in true righteousness and holiness.

EPHESIANS 6:13 [13]Therefore take up the whole armor of God, that you may be able to withstand in the evil day, and having done all, to stand firm.

PHILIPPIANS 4:8 Finally, brothers, whatever is true, whatever is honorable, whatever is just, whatever is pure, whatever is lovely, whatever is commendable, if there is any excellence, if there is anything worthy of praise, think about these things.

COLOSSIANS 3:1-2 [1]If then you have been raised with Christ, seek the things that are above, where Christ is, seated at the right hand of God. [2]Set your minds on things that are above, not on things that are on earth.

COLOSSIANS 3:10 Put on the new self, which is being renewed in knowledge after the image of its creator.

HEBREWS 11:16 And without faith it is impossible to please him, for whoever would draw near to God must believe that he exists and that he rewards those who seek him.

Continued on Next Page...

We take captive
EVERY THOUGHT
to make it
OBEDIENT
TO CHRIST

II. FIGHTING SPECIFIC IDOLS

A. FIGHTING AN IDOL OF CONTROL WITH THE TRUTHS OF TRUST AND STEWARDSHIP

TRUTHS OF TRUST:

ISAIAH 41:10 Fear not, for I am with you; be not dismayed, for I am your God; I will strengthen you, I will help you, I will uphold you with my righteous right hand.

JEREMIAH 17:7–8 [7]Blessed is the man who trusts in the LORD, whose trust is the LORD. [8]He is like a tree planted by water, that sends out its roots by the stream, and does not fear when heat comes, for its leaves remain green, and is not anxious in the year of drought, for it does not cease to bear fruit.

PROVERBS 3:5–6 [5]Trust in the LORD with all your heart, and do not lean on your own understanding. [6]In all your ways acknowledge him, and he will make straight your paths.

MATTHEW 6:25, 33–34 [25]"Therefore I tell you, do not be anxious about your life, what you will eat or what you will drink, nor about your body, what you will put on. Is not life more than food, and the body more than clothing? . . . [33]But seek first the kingdom of God and his righteousness, and all these things will be added to you [34]Therefore do not be anxious about tomorrow, for tomorrow will be anxious for itself. Sufficient for the day is its own trouble.

JOHN 14:1 [Jesus speaking] "Let not your hearts be troubled. Believe in God; believe also in me."

PHILIPPIANS 4:6–7 [6]Do not be anxious about anything but in everything by prayer and supplication with thanksgiving let your requests be made known to God. [7]And the peace of God, which surpasses all understanding, will guard your hearts and your minds i Christ Jesus.

1 PETER 5:6–7 [6]Humble yourselves, therefore, under the mighty hand of God so that at the proper time he may exalt you, [7]casting all your anxieties on him, because he cares for you.

TRUTHS OF STEWARDSHIP:

GENESIS 2:15 The LORD God took the man and put h in the garden of Eden to work it and keep it.

PSALM 24:1-2 The earth is the LORD's and the fullness thereof, the world and those who dwell therein, [2] for he has founded it upon the seas and established it upon t rivers.

LUKE 12:48 Everyone to whom much was given, of him much will be required, and from him to whom th entrusted much, they will demand the more.

1 PETER 4:10 As each has received a gift, use it to se one another, as good stewards of God's varied grace

B. FIGHTING AN IDOL OF SIGNIFICANCE WITH THE TRUTHS OF FEARING GOD AND HUMILITY

TRUTHS OF FEARING GOD:

PSALM 97:7 All worshipers of images are put to shame, who make their boast in worthless idols; worship him [the Lord], all you gods!

PSALM 113:4–6 [4]The LORD is high above all nations, and his glory above the heavens! [5]Who is like the LORD our God, who is seated on high, [6]who looks far down on the heavens and the earth?

PSALM 118:8 It is better to take refuge in the Lord than to trust in man.

PROVERBS 1:7 The fear of the LORD is the beginning of knowledge.

ECCLESIASTES 12:13 The end of the matter; all has been heard. Fear God and keep his commandments, for this is the whole duty of man.

COLOSSIANS 3:23 Whatever you do, work heartily, as for the Lord and not for men.

TRUTHS OF HUMILITY:

1 SAMUEL 16:7 For the LORD sees not as man sees: man looks on the outward appearance, but the LORD looks on the heart.

PSALM 34:2 My soul makes its boast in the LORD; let the humble hear and be glad.

PSALM 147:10–11 [10]His delight is not in the strength of the horse, nor his pleasure in the legs of a man, [11]but the Lord takes pleasure in those who fear him, in those who hope in his steadfast love.

JEREMIAH 9:23–24 [23]Thus says the LORD: "Let not the wise man boast in his wisdom, let not the mighty man boast in his might, let not the rich man boast in his riches, [24]but let him who boasts boast in this, that he understands and knows me, that I am the LORD who practices steadfast love, justice, and righteousness in the earth. For in these things I delight, declares the LORD."

ROMANS 12:3 For by the grace given to me I say to everyone among you not to think of himself more highly than he ought to think, but to think with sober judgment, each according to the measure of faith that God has assigned.

1 PETER 5:5–6 [5]Clothe yourselves, all of you, with humility toward one another, for "God opposes the proud but gives grace to the humble." [6]Humble yourselves, therefore, under the mighty hand of God so that at the proper time he may exalt you.

C. FIGHTING AN IDOL OF COMFORT WITH THE TRUTHS OF GODLY AMBITION, SELF-SACRIFICE, AND GOD HIMSELF

TRUTHS OF GODLY AMBITION:

COLOSSIANS 3:23 Whatever you do, work heartily, as for the Lord and not for men.

HEBREWS 12:1–2 [1]Let us also lay aside every weight, and sin which clings so closely, and let us run with endurance the race that is set before us, [2]looking to Jesus, the founder and perfecter of our faith, who for the joy that was set before him endured the cross, despising the shame, and is seated at the right hand of the throne of God.

TRUTHS OF SELF-SACRIFICE:

1 CORINTHIANS 9:24–27 [24]Do you not know that in a race all the runners run, but only one receives the prize? So run that you may obtain it. [25]Every athlete exercises self-control in all things. They do it to receive a perishable wreath, but we an imperishable. [26]So I do not run aimlessly; I do not box as one beating the air. [27]But I discipline my body and keep it under control, lest after preaching to others I myself should be disqualified.

1 TIMOTHY 5:8 But if anyone does not provide for his relatives, and especially for members of his household, he has denied the faith and is worse than an unbeliever.

TRUTHS OF GOD HIMSELF:

JOSHUA 1:9 Be strong and courageous. Do not be frightened, and do not be dismayed, for the LORD your God is with you wherever you go.

PSALM 16:11 You make known to me the path of life; in your presence there is fullness of joy; at your right hand are pleasures forevermore.

PSALM 37:4 Delight yourself in the LORD, and he will give you the desires of your heart.

PROVERBS 19:21 Many are the plans in the mind of a man, but it is the purpose of the Lord that will stand.

PHILIPPIANS 3:8 Indeed, I count everything as loss because of the surpassing worth of knowing Christ Jesus my Lord. For his sake I have suffered the loss of all things and count them as rubbish, in order that I may gain Christ.

***See page 78 for Scripture to help you battle porn and sexual lust**

**** All Scriptures are ESV**

War in the Wilderness

The Situation

Jesus had been fasting forty days in the desert, preparing to begin His earthly ministry. He was extremely weak, hungry, and thirsty. Satan attacked Him in His most vulnerable state.

Satan then took Jesus to the holy city and had Him stand on the highest point of the temple.

Satan took Jesus to a very high mountain and showed Him all the kingdoms of the world and their splendor.

Jesus, our model for Authentic Manhood, faced temptation just as we do today.

In fact, in Hebrews 4:15, the Bible says regarding Jesus:
"For we do not have a high priest who is unable to sympathize with our weaknesses, but we have one ***who has been tempted in every way, just as we are***—yet was without sin. Let us then approach the throne of grace with confidence, so that we may receive mercy and find grace to help us in our time of need."

The Book of Matthew records Jesus facing temptations that are common to every man—and emerging victorious.

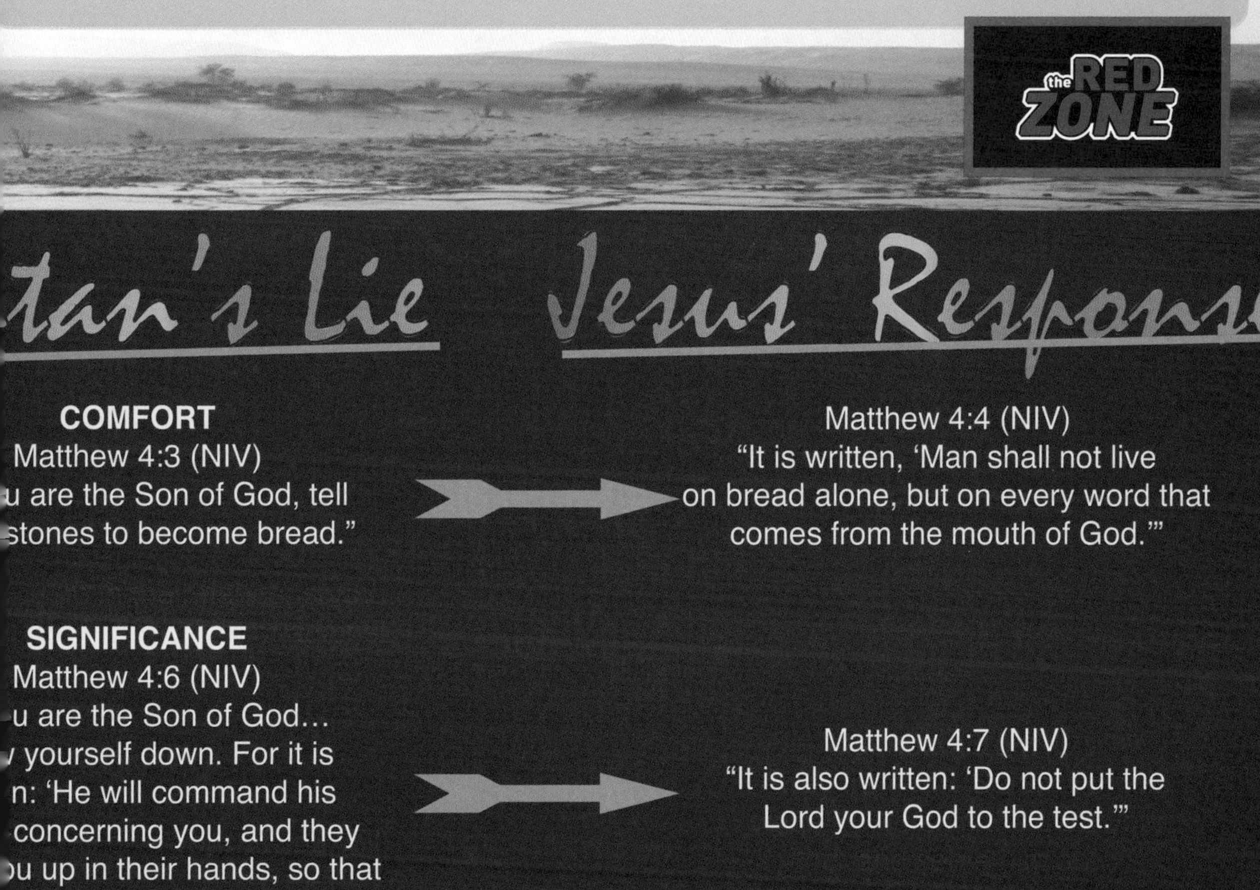

the RED ZONE
tan's Lie
Jesus' Response
COMFORT
Matthew 4:3 (NIV)
u are the Son of God, tell
stones to become bread."
Matthew 4:4 (NIV)
"It is written, 'Man shall not live on bread alone, but on every word that comes from the mouth of God.'"
SIGNIFICANCE
Matthew 4:6 (NIV)
u are the Son of God…
yourself down. For it is
n: 'He will command his
concerning you, and they
u up in their hands, so that
not strike your foot against
a stone.'"
Matthew 4:7 (NIV)
"It is also written: 'Do not put the Lord your God to the test.'"
CONTROL
Matthew 4:9 (NIV)
I will give you…if you will
down and worship me."
Matthew 4:10 (NIV)
"Away from me, Satan! For it is written: 'Worship the Lord your God, and serve him only.'"

SCRIPTURE REFERENCES

John 10:10 (ESV) "I came that they may have life and have it abundantly."

Romans 5:8 (ESV) "But God shows his love for us in that while we were still sinners, Christ died for us."

Romans 8:28 (ESV) "And we know that for those who love God all things work together for good, for those who are called according to his purpose."

Romans 12:2 (ESV) "Do not be conformed to this world, but be transformed by the renewal of your mind, that by testing you may discern what is the will of God, what is good and acceptable and perfect."

Ephesians 2:4–5 (ESV) "But God, being rich in mercy, because of the great love with which he loved us, even when we were dead in our trespasses, made us alive together with Christ—by grace you have been saved."

Colossians 3:2 (ESV) "Set your minds on things that are above, not on things that are on earth."

Hebrews 10:10 (ESV) "We have been sanctified through the offering of the body of Jesus Christ once for all."

Hebrews 12:2 (ESV) "[Look] to Jesus, the founder and perfecter of our faith, who for the joy that was set before him endured the cross, despising the shame, and is seated at the right hand of the throne of God."

James 5:16 (ESV) "Therefore, confess your sins to one another and pray for one another, that you may be healed. The prayer of a righteous person has great power as it is working."

SUPPORTING RESOURCES

Piper, John. *Future Grace. Revised Edition.* Multnomah Press, 2012. *In this book, John Piper examines the power of faith in God's promises to extinguish the lure of sin. See also the abbreviated version:* Battling Unbelief: Defeating Sin with Superior Pleasure (Multnomah, 2007).

Bridges, Jerry and Bob Bevington. *The Bookends of the Christian Life.* Crossway, 2009. *This short book very helpfully discusses (1) the importance of "the righteousness of Christ" and (2) "the power of the Holy Spirit" for living the Christian life.*

Dieter, Melvin E., ed. *Five Views of Sanctification.* Zondervan, 1996. *This volume is an overview of different Christian views of sanctification. It assumes an intermediate knowledge of theology.*

** The content in the resources above does not necessarily reflect the opinion of Authentic Manhood. Readers should utilize these resources but form their own opinions.*

SESSION **FOUR** | Training Guide

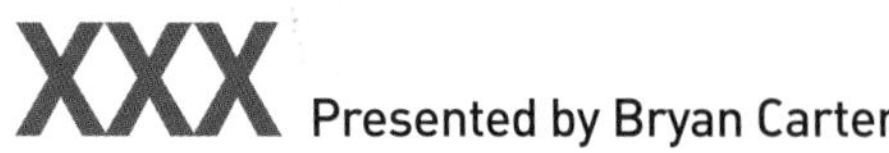

XXX Presented by Bryan Carter

I. INTRODUCTION

1. Whether you're age 25 or age 75—if you're a man—then sexual ____________________ is a part of your battle and most likely your daily battle.

2. When pursued according to God's "noble pathway," sexuality can be healthy and healing. When pursued according to Satan's "shadow pathway," it only leads to hiding, deep darkness, and eventually a personal prison.

3. Perceived anonymity and pervasive ____________________ have made pornography a bigger problem than ever before.

II. SUSCEPTIBLE BRAINS AND DISCONNECTED HEARTS

1. Susceptible Brains

   - God intended for us to ____________________ in the bodily form of our wife and for her to enjoy our enjoyment.
   - When a man views pornography, pleasure chemicals are released in his brain in amounts that far exceed normal levels.
   - You quickly build up a tolerance to the same old stuff you've already seen and to get the old high you'll have to ____________________ the boundaries.
   - We are not playing with something harmless or safe. This stuff is liquid nitrogen.
   - You are not ____________________. This should strike shame at its root because we are all in the same boat and have the same capacity for this stuff.

2. Disconnected Hearts

   - Struggles with pornography and sex betray a deeper need in us—a deep need for ____________________ with God and others.

- Show me a man connected to God and trustworthy men and I'll show you a man nobly fighting the battle with lust.

III. THE NOBLE FIGHT AGAINST LUST: APPLYING OUR "BATTLE PLAN"

1. We've got to admit the sin and pursue ruthless ______________________ beginning with ourselves and then with trustworthy men.

   - When we remove the mask, we've taken the first step in trumping the need to medicate. It breaks the cycle and provides space for truth and hope to invade.

2. Identify the broken ________________________ of pornography.

3. Now we get to move from the broken promises of lust to a vision for something better.

   - The power to say "no" to pornography is in being convinced that God Himself and the pathway of Authentic Manhood is more __________________________ and more lasting than the lure of lust.

   - When you begin renewing your mind by turning to God's truths, you'll find an entirely new strength in your heart.

   - We must load our minds and hearts with the ammunition of Scripture's more satisfying promises.

IV. FIGHT THE BATTLE

1. Pursue ____________________ with God.

- "Every man who knocks on the door of a brothel is looking for God."
  -G.K. Chesterton

2. Pursue heart-level community with other men and your wife. (James 5:16)

   "The pursuit of purity is not about the suppression of lust, but about the reorientation of one's life to a larger goal." - Deitrich Bonhoeffer

3. When you're actively pursuing a bigger God-vision for your life, you'll find your passion for Him and His vision increasing, and your attention to lust decreasing.

4. Run to ______________________ with all your heart, store His promises in your mind and heart, and rest in His grace and His infinite pleasures.

DISCUSSION / REFLECTION QUESTIONS

1. How can understanding the truth about how the male brain operates help you?

2. Reflect on this statement: "Show me a man disconnected from God, from his wife, and from others, and I'll show you a man either struggling with, or extremely vulnerable to, sexual temptation. But, show me a man connected to God, his wife, and trustworthy men, and I'll show you a man who has a chance to fight the noble fight." Are you currently experiencing heart-level connection with God, your spouse (if you are married), and trustworthy men? Discuss.

3. Which of the 3 Deep Idols (control, significance, and comfort) is at the root of your battle with sexual temptation? What false promise can lust use to lure you (escape, validation, power, acceptance, comfort)?

4. Share what you felt after experiencing Bryan Carter's transparency as he shared about his struggle with pornography. Do you have the freedom to be that transparent with other trustworthy men who can fight the battle with you?

5. Write down (on page 68) and share with your group your one or two STRATEGIC MOVES that you need to make in order to apply what you've learned in this session.

AUTHENTIC MANHOOD

YOUR STRATEGIC MOVE

RESOURCES ON THE FOLLOWING PAGES:

decide for
OVERCOMING POR

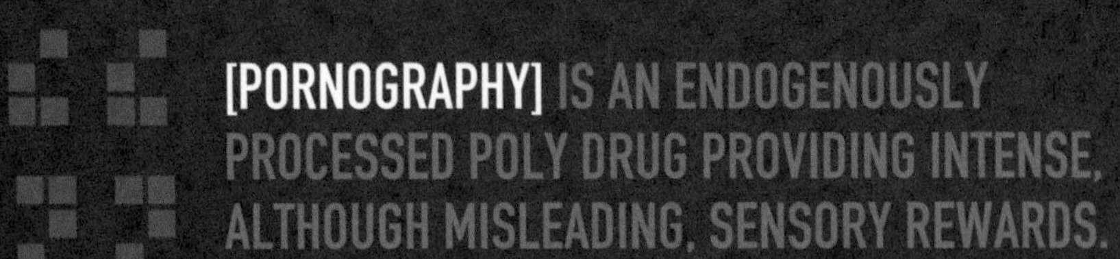
[PORNOGRAPHY] IS AN ENDOGENOUSLY
PROCESSED POLY DRUG PROVIDING INTENSE,
ALTHOUGH MISLEADING, SENSORY REWARDS.

by Craig Gross

pornography is like a drug

SIMILAR TO OTHER SUBSTANCES OF ABUSE, IT ALTERS OUR BRAIN FUNCTION, AND IN THAT SENSE, IT IS A DRUG. In her 2003 report prepared for the Department of Justice, researcher Judith A. Reisman wrote,

> *"[Pornography] is an endogenously processed poly drug providing intense, although misleading, sensory rewards."*

While we may not ingest or inject pornography into our systems to get a high (like we would with, say, cocaine or heroin), pornography use triggers the brain to produce neurochemicals that give us highs similar to other drugs. Pornography, Reisman writes, kick-starts "endogenous LSD, adrenaline/norepinephrine, morphine like neurochemicals for a hormonal flood, a 'rush' allegedly analogous to the rush attained using various street drugs."

This may not come as much of a surprise to many men who use pornography. If there were no rush, no thrill in either seeking it or viewing it, then there would be no purpose in pursuing it. It would lose its meaning and become pointless.

Do people who are recovering from addictions to substances like heroin and methamphetamine use the word sobriety as part of their healing process? Yes, they do. Should we use that word in our discussion of compulsive pornography use?

yes, we should.

IF YOU ARE STRUGGLING WITH COMPULSIVE USE OF PORNOGRAPHY,

if you find either that you cannot control your behavior with pornography use or that without using pornography you are depressed or agitated (the classic definition of dependence), now is a good time to accept the word sobriety in your discussion of abstaining from using pornography. With the adoption of that word, you are also adopting the other connotations that come along with it: pornography is a destructive drug, and you want to quit using it.

All the dissecting, analyzing, discussing, and reading you may do in trying to overcome your addiction to pornography are pointless unless you are committed to seeking your sobriety.

sounds easy, right?

Just decide you want to stop using porn, figure out your life's purpose, and start heading toward it. Of course, it is much more difficult than it sounds. But let us take a second to flip this around. Instead of thinking that we need t commit to sobriety by a sheer act of force, like a 150-pound offensive linema hitting a 350-pound linebacker head-on in the chest, there is a way to think of this commitment in leveraged terms, more like the lineman hitting that linebacker low, in his legs, where the size disadvantage disappears and the linebacker is brought down to the ground.

MICHAEL JORDAN WOULD HAVE BEEN JUST ANOTHER BASKETBALL PLAYER IF HE HADN'T UNDERSTOOD THE NEED TO BUILD UP AND RELY ON HIS TEAMMATES TO WIN CHAMPIONSHIPS.

MOST MEN WANT TO BE LEADERS. They want to be the great deciders, the ones wh overcome, the champions. An unfortunate offshoot of this very noble instinct that we do not like being told what to do. We make the decisions, not someon else. And if we have made a mistake, like letting ourselves become addicted t something unhealthy, it can be hard to admit that we have screwed up. After all, leaders do not make mistakes, right?

But what kind of leader never listens to opposing views? What kind of leader does not seek help or admit fault? Michael Jordan would have been just another basketball player if he had not understood the need to build up and rely on his teammates to win championships. Winston Churchill's England could have been over-run by the Germans in 1941 if Churchill hadn' recognized how weak his country was financially and how they needed Ameri and President Roosevelt's help. Roosevelt put it best when he wrote, "It is common sense to take a method and try it. If it fails, admit it frankly and try another. But above all, try something."

HE POINT IN THESE EXAMPLES IS TWOFOLD:

rst, a commitment to sobriety is a lot more difficult—e would argue impossible—without first admitting that ou are not only powerless over your addiction but also owerless within the universe; and second, if you really ant to be a leader, a decider, a champion, you have the pportunity, right now, to make decisions for yourself stead of letting someone else make them for you.

you really want to enjoy all the wonderful benefits at come with your faith (including the power of Christ overcome painful struggles), you need to choose to ccept the fact that Christ died on the cross to set you ee in order to recieve His grace and the power that is truth can bring to you. He died as the once-and-r-all atonement so that the pressure you may feel om having made a bad decision or the pressure you ay feel to always make the right decision can be lifted that you can experience peace, happiness, and joy. ccept this gift. Revel in it. As Jesus said in John 10:10, he thief comes only to steal and kill and destroy; ave come that [you] may have life, and have it to e full."

Part of having life to the full is the opportunity to make decisions for yourself. God loves you, and, yes, He loves being loved in return, but He wants real love, a love that comes willingly, from your heart, uncoerced. When we do not choose Him, or do not choose to make decisions that honor Him, we're choosing death, theft, and destruction.

Good leadership starts with a decision to do the right thing. The true champions want to pursue real truth. Truth that will renew their minds and begin their transformation to be the man God has made them to be. It all begins with the courage and the willingness to decide for yourself that your faith and trust is in the grace and truth of Jesus, the giver of the full life. The one whose truth can replace the lies. Whose grace offers the real joy and meaning that your soul desires.

As men who wish to be the great leaders, the great deciders, the champions, admitting fault, trading in the lies of porn for God's truth is not only admirable, it's life changing.

image from http://creativity103.com

AIG GROSS IS THE FOUNDER OF XXXCHURCH.COM WHICH STARTED IN 2002. It has become e largest website online helping those caught up in pornography or sexual . He has written several books and speaks across the globe. His latest book ***Open—What Happens When You Get Real, Get Honest and Get Accountable***. ore information can be found at www.getopen.com.

THE FIRST OF THE FOUR REALITIES IS PURSUING RUTHLESS HONESTY IN THE COMPANY OF TRUSTWORTHY MEN.

HEALING COMMUNITY

BY TRAYLOR LOVVORN

WE ARE HERE TO CONNECT AT WEAKNESS INSTEAD OF TRYING TO IMPRESS WITH STRENGTH.

EACH WEEK I OPEN A GATHERING OF MEN whose deep idols have surfaced as an addiction to sex and pornography with the reminder that "we are here to connect in weakness instead of trying to impress in strength." Each week I witness men engaging at the heart level with other men with their true, authentic self instead of pretending with the pose that is often more safe and familiar.

IN VOLUME 1 OF "33," I SHARED MY STORY OF LOSING MY WIFE AND FOUR CHILDREN DUE TO MY SEXUAL ADDICTION. I shared that a "journey into authenticity" after our divorce ultimately made reconciliation possible for us. For years I had struggled in isolation, desperately trying to overcome my struggle with sexual sin on my own so that no one would know my shameful secret. I did not realize that by isolating, I was taking a path away from God's promised healing. In James 5:16 we discover God's formula for genuine healing:

"Therefore, confess your sins to one another and pray for one another, that you may be healed."

Even though I had heard the truth for years as it related to the deep idols of my heart, I was attempting to apply that truth to my life in a dark, isolated corner. My isolation fed the lie that I was the only Christian man struggling with sexual sin and that God had about had enough of my bad choices. It was not until I began to step out of isolation and toward other safe men that my core lies were exposed and challenged. Authentic community provided the context for me to tell the truth about myself and receive love and acceptance from others instead of the rejection that I feared.

VOLUME 3 IS PROVIDING YOU WITH GREAT TEACHING ON HOW TO RECOGNIZE AND DEAL WITH YOUR DEEP HEART IDOLS. But do not make the mistake of trying to apply these truths in isolation. The first of the four realities is pursuing ruthless honesty in the company of trustworthy men. This type of community does not happen by accident, but requires risk and intentional effort. You might get hurt in the process. It is messy because each of our stories are messy. But guys, it is vital to becoming the authentic men we were created to be.

I WANT YOU TO HEAR FROM TWO OF THE MEN I HAVE THE PRIVILEGE OF DOING LIFE WITH EACH WEEK. I KNOW GREG AND ROGER'S STRENGTHS AND THEY KNOW MINE. BUT WE ALSO KNOW EACH OTHER'S WEAKNESSES, INSECURITIES, AND THE LIES WE ARE SO QUICK TO BELIEVE.

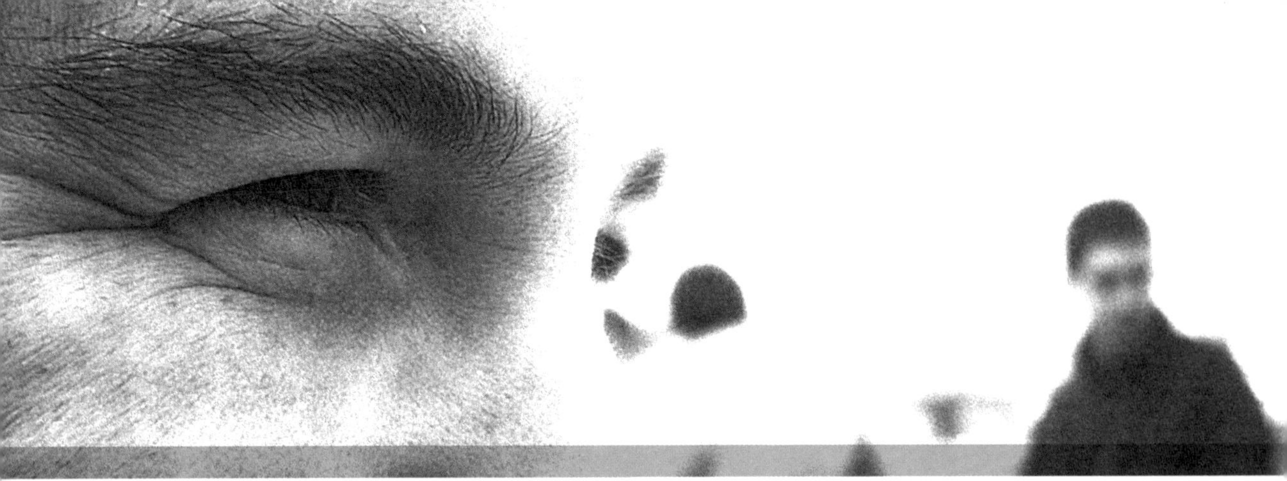

GREG'S STORY

I BECAME A CHRISTIAN AT AGE 6, grew up in the church, was heavily involved in music, graduated from Bible college, married a missionary, and served the church as a worship pastor. Through most of that time, I also struggled with sexual temptation that manifested itself through pornography use, masturbation, and fantasy that eventually developed into an addiction to sex.

GROWING UP IN A CONSERVATIVE CHURCH SETTING, I LEARNED THAT THERE WERE THINGS THAT "GOOD CHRISTIANS" DID NOT DO, AND ALSO DID NOT TALK ABOUT.

When I began to be aware of my sexuality, I did not feel that I had a safe outlet to work through what I was feeling, so I learned to isolate and to navigate through my experiences as best I could on my own. Through this practice, I also developed the habit of using masturbation and porn to "medicate" all the things that were wrong in life—stresses, fears, hurts—rather than learning to work through them in healthy ways.

By the time I married, these habits were firmly established. I already had secrets I was hiding from my wife. She did not know I had struggled with porn and masturbation, and I naively believed that marriage would fix these issues, simply making them unnecessary. I thought things would self-correct.

But since my idols had not been identified or dealt with, nothing changed. Marriage did not make my life perfect, and as I continued to experience negative emotion, I continued to run back to the old medicine. Over the next several years, my use of pornography intensified, and led to a growing fantasy life. What I did not know was that these practice were paving the way for physical adultery. What started as a visit for a sensual massag eventually turned into anonymous sexual encounters.

Over a six year period, my cycle of will-powe failure, acting out, shame, and trying again continued over and over again. Eventually, I came to believe that each time I felt the trig and urge to act out, it was an unavoidable conclusion. So, I became hopeless and pragmatic—"Let us just get this over with."

WITH NO HOPE THAT THINGS WOULD EVER CHAN I CONCLUDED THAT I COULD NEVER COME CLEAN

I believed I had done too much and that it would ruin my life and my family's lives as well. But God loved me too much to allow m to continue to self-destruct, and caused me to be exposed. While I did lose a lot (my job some friends, etc), He saved and healed my marriage and family. Since early 2009, He h been leading me through a redemptive path recovery and sobriety that is grounded in th gospel of Jesus Christ and intimate commu with other men who share this struggle.

A huge component of my journey has been involvement in a community of other men walking recovery with me. Just like isolatio breeds and strengthens the hold of addicti authentic community releases that hold as reminds me that I am not alone. This strug is not unique to me. Walking in community allows me to share and receive the hope of the gospel, and to actively identify and figh the lies I often believe about myself. We we never meant to alone.

ROGER'S STORY

WHEN MY WIFE FIRST LEARNED OF MY ADDICTION, she was devastated. I told her that I would do whatever I had to do to fix this. And I would go to work trying to change and "fix" my sex addiction. When she saw me really trying, she would become comfortable and think everything was okay. I would become comfortable too. Then I would start acting out again and eventually she would find out again.

AFTER GOING THROUGH THIS CYCLE SEVERAL TIMES, I CAME TO REALIZE THAT I HAD A PROBLEM.

I was making my wife happy by going to groups, but I was really not participating. Again, things got comfortable and I fell off of the wagon again.

Finally, I started going to a therapist and exploring what was really causing this addictive behavior. The most important thing I learned was that it was not about the sex. The sex was almost secondary. Some people choose to deal with the pain of the past through alcohol or drugs. My chosen medication was pornography and sex. That was eye-opening to me to know that there were deeper issues I needed to explore. It quickly became apparent that the lies I was believing about my deep idols started in childhood.

I had an very distant father. He always told me that he loved me but I felt unimportant to him. He was a carpenter and was always busy with work. I had an older brother who would assist him with projects. I always wanted to help, but I was never allowed. My dad came up with a compromise: I would be paid like my brother, but not to help...to stay out of the way.

I felt like my dad taught my brother how to be a man, but I had to figure out what this meant on my own. Because of this, I have always felt inferior around other men. What I found was that any time that shame would surface, I would medicate with my drug of choice: pornography and sex. By medicating, I was getting the attention, gratification, and affirmation I needed. But it did not last.

Finally, God brought me to the realization that I was getting nowhere handling things on my own. He led me to safe community. He introduced me to people who had struggles similar to my own. The groups were different than those I had experienced before—there was a sense of hope. As I became more involved, I discovered that I did have a Father who wanted me to be around Him. He loved me regardless of what I had done. I was His beloved son.

MY BREAKTHROUGH CAME WHEN I REALIZED THAT COMMUNITY WAS MORE THAN JUST GOING TO MEETINGS. COMMUNITY MEANT PURSUING OTHER MEN AND RISKING LETTING THEM KNOW MY STORY AS I LISTENED INTENTLY TO THEIRS. THIS HAS BEEN THE KEY TO MY JOURNEY—TO BE PART OF A COMMUNITY WHERE I CAN SAY THINGS ALOUD WITHOUT THE RISK OF BEING JUDGED OR SHAMED AND WHERE THE LIES OF MY PAST ARE MET WITH THE TRUTH OF THE GOSPEL.

IT'S IN COMMUNITY WHERE THE LIES WE ARE TOLD ARE MET WITH THE TRUTH OF THE GOSPEL

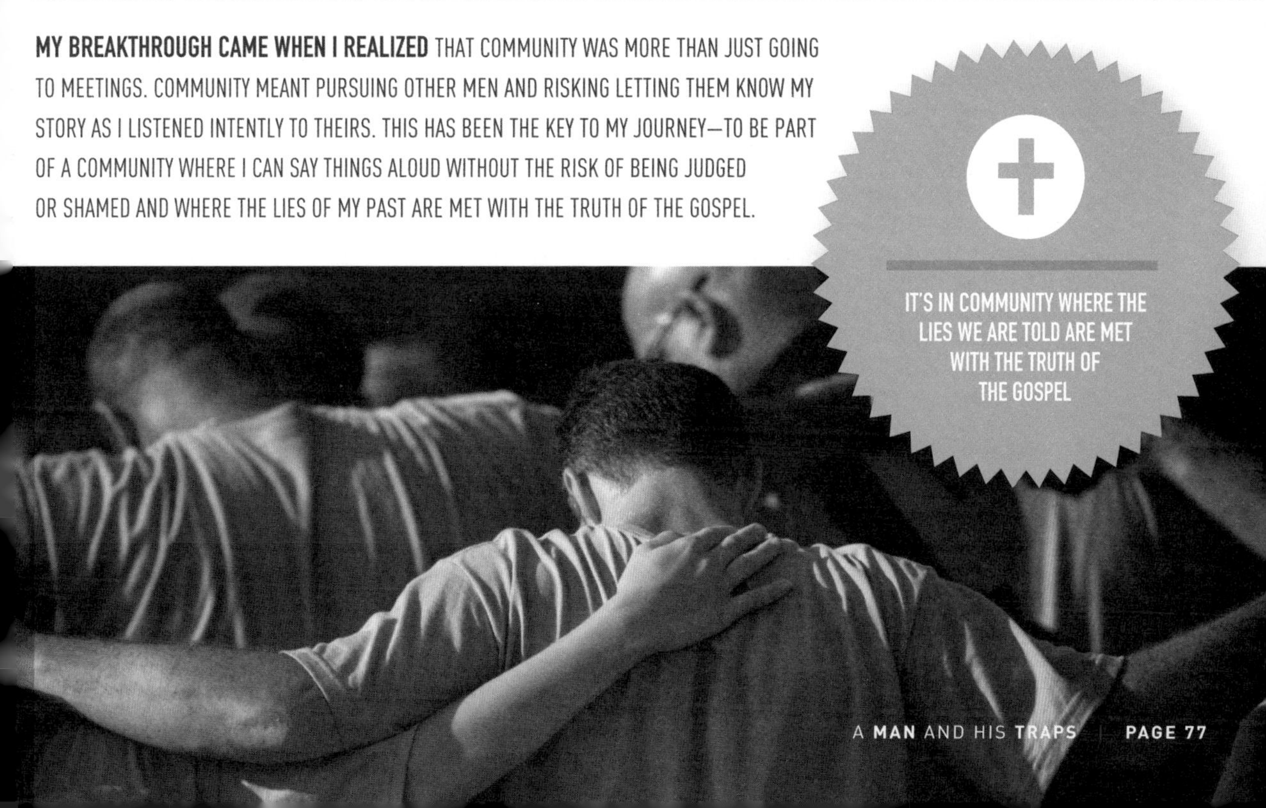

AMMUNITION to HELP YOU BATTLE PORN & SEXUAL LUST

Job 31:1 (ESV) [Job speaking] "I have made a covenant with my eyes; how then could I gaze at a virgin?"

Proverbs 5:18-20 (ESV) "Rejoice in the wife of your youth, a lovely deer, a graceful doe. Let her breasts fill you at all times with delight; be intoxicated always in her love. Why should you be intoxicated, my son, with a forbidden woman and embrace the bosom of an adulteress?"

Proverbs 6:32 (ESV) He who commits adultery lacks sense; he who does it destroys himself.

Matthew 5:27-28 (ESV) [Jesus speaking] "You have heard that it was said, 'You shall not commit adultery.' But I say to you that everyone who looks at a woman with lustful intent has already committed adultery with her in his heart."

Matthew 6:22-23 (ESV) [Jesus speaking] "The eye is the lamp of the body. So, if your eye is healthy, your whole body will be full of light, but if your eye is bad, your whole body will be full of darkness."

Romans 13:13-14 (ESV) "Let us walk properly as in the daytime, not in orgies and drunkenness, not in sexual immorality and sensuality, not in quarreling and jealousy. But put on the Lord Jesus Christ, and make no provision for the flesh, to gratify its desires."

1 Corinthians 6:18-20 (ESV) "Flee from sexual immorality. Every other sin a person commits is outside the body, but the sexually immoral person sins against his own body. Or do you not know that your body is a temple of the Holy Spirit within you, whom you have from God? You are not your own, for you were bought with a price. So glorify God in your body."

Colossians 3:5 (ESV) "Put to death therefore what is earthly in you: sexual immorality, impurity, passion, evil desire, and covetousness, which is idolatry."

1 Thessalonians 4:3-4 (ESV) "For this is the will of God, your sanctification: that you abstain from sexual immorality; that each one of you know how to control his own body in holiness and honor."

Hebrews 13:4 (ESV) "Let marriage be held in honor among all, and let the marriage bed be undefiled, for God will judge the sexually immoral and adulterous."

ADDITIONAL RESOURCES TO HELP YOU BATTLE PORN AND SEXUAL LUST

XXX CHURCH And X3watch

XXXchurch.com exists to help people of all ages who have an addiction to pornography. XXXchurch offers addiction recovery resources for men. We prevail through awareness, prevention and recovery.

X3watch is an accountability software program that helps with online integrity. Whenever you access a website that contains inappropriate or pornographic material, the program records the site, time, and date you visited. A person of your choice (an accountability partner) will receive an email or text message containing a list of all these sites.

ROUTE 1520

Route1520 is built on the firm belief that individuals cannot change through mere willpower or simply learning Biblical principles and trying to carry them out. We believe that change takes place in community as we take the gospel of Jesus Christ more deeply into our understanding and into our hearts. Visit: Route1520.com

CAPSTONE TREATMENT CENTER

The Capstone Mission is to provide a highly effective treatment experience to give residents and families the best opportunity to make a paradigm shift in their life's direction – to recovery. The success of our treatment approach is in the synergy of professionally excellent therapy in a Christ-centered environment, delivered by professionally excellent individuals who live Christ-centered lives. The Capstone therapy experience treats residents' addiction(s) as well as the underlying psychological-emotional-relational-spiritual problems. As far as God is concerned, Capstone takes residents where they are, from atheist to devout believer, and simply cultivates spirituality from that point, at the resident's pace, as we develop relationships and implement our Core Model of therapy. Visit: capstonetreatmentcenter.com

---

PORN AGAIN CHRISTIAN By Mark Driscoll

A frank discussion on porn and masturbation. This short book (50 pages) is a hard-hitter that gets straight to the point. The text doesn't offer any superficial antics. Rather it addresses the heart of the matter—the Christian life has no place for pornography & sexual sin.

REAL MARRIAGE By Mark and Grace Driscoll

Pastor Mark Driscoll and his wife, Grace, share how they have struggled and how they have found healing through the power of the only reliable source: the Bible. They believe friendship is fundamental to marriage but not easy to maintain. So they offer practical advice on how to make your spouse your best friend—and keep it that way. And they know from experience that sex-related issues need to be addressed directly.

EVERY MAN'S BATTLE By Stephen Arterburn, Fred Stoeker, Mike Yorkey

From movies and television, to print media and the Internet, men are constantly faced with the assault of sensual images. It is impossible to avoid such temptations... but, thankfully, not impossible to confront them and gain victory over them! With extensive updates for a new generation, this phenomenal bestseller shares the stories of dozens who have escaped the trap of sexual immorality and presents a practical, detailed plan for any man who desires sexual integrity

SEXUAL SANITY FOR MEN By David White

Written for Christian men struggling with any form of sexual brokenness, this resource helps men understand that sexual sin starts in their minds and hearts and shows them how knowing Christ breaks their chains, builds spiritual brotherhood, and helps them take practical steps to re-create their minds in a God-focused direction.

SEX AND THE SUPREMACY OF CHRIST By John Piper and Justin Taylor

The Bible has a way of shocking us. If Americans could still blush, we might blush at the words, "Rejoice in the wife of your youth, a lovely deer, a graceful doe. Let her breasts fill you at all times with delight; be intoxicated always in her love" (Proverbs 5:18-19).

But, of course, sin always tries to trash God's gifts. So we can't just celebrate sex for what God made it to be; we have to fight what sin turned it into. The contributors to this unique volume encourage you to do both: celebrate and struggle.

Shedding Light on a GLOBAL PANDEMIC

30%
Percentage of all web traffic that involves pornography.

20
Length of time, in minutes, the average guest spends on the site per visit.

$2.84 billion
Porn industry revenue, annually, from the United States alone.

11
The average age at which a child first sees porn online.

4.4 billion
Average page views, monthly, of one of the web's leading porn sites.

67%
Percent of men who say viewing porn is acceptable behavior.

$4.9 billion
Annual global porn industry revenue.

28,258
# of porn viewers, on average, each second.

Sunday
The most popular day of the week for viewing porn.

The numbers are staggering.
Men of all ages, ethnicities, professions, and income levels are willingly infecting their hearts and minds with images that are addictive, destructive, and in some cases, criminal.

116,000
Average online searches for child pornography each day.

21%
Percent of teenage girls who admit to texting a nude photo of themselves.

12-17
Age range of the largest demographic of porn consumers.

70%
Percentage of men, ages 18-34, who visit porn sites in a typical month.

70%
Percent of Christian men who view porn regularly

20%
Percent of men who admit to watching porn online at work.

69%
Percent of pastors who say porn has adversely affected the church.

Sources: Medical Daily, January 2013; CBN News; Journey to Freedom, Everyday Christian by Chad Barrett, October 2011; UnitedFamiliesInternational.wordpress.com; Baptist Press, LifeWay Research and Education Database; Daily Mail, August 2012; DigitalJournal.com, "Pornography: Everybody is watching it" by John Thomas Didymus, April 2012

SCRIPTURE REFERENCES

Mark 12:29–31 (ESV) Jesus answered, "The most important [commandment] is, 'Hear, O Israel: The Lord our God, the Lord is one. And you shall love the Lord your God with all your heart and with all your soul and with all your mind and with all your strength.' The second [commandment] is this: 'You shall love your neighbor as yourself.' There is no other commandment greater than these."

SUPPORTING RESOURCES

Piper, John. "Faith in Future Grace vs. Lust." Pages 329–340 in Future Grace. Revised Edition. Colorado Springs: Multnomah, 2012. This chapter is especially helpful in understanding the importance of fighting lust with the more satisfying promises of scripture.

Cusick, Michael John. *Surfing for God: Discovering the Divine Desire beneath Sexual Sin Struggle*. Nashville: Thomas Nelson, 2012. This book is one of the better book-length treatments of how to battle sexual temptation and lust.

Gilkerson, Luke. *Your Brain on Porn: 5 Proven Ways Pornography Warps Your Mind and 3 Biblical Ways to Renew It.* Covenant Eyes E-Book, 2011. Online: www.covenanteyes.com. Gilkerson provides a very readable overview of recent research on the effects of pornography on the brain.

Whitney, Donald S. *Spiritual Disciplines for the Christian Life*. NavPress, 1997. The spiritual disciplines are time-tested Christian practices for building intimacy with God. In this volume, Donald Whitney provides an introduction and guide to practicing the spiritual disciplines.

** The content in the resources above does not necessarily reflect the opinion of Authentic Manhood. Readers should utilize these resources but form their own opinions.*

Control

SESSION **FIVE** | Training Guide

Control Presented by John Bryson

I. INTRODUCTION[1]

1.

2. In our final two sessions, we are going to continue the practical application of our biblical "Battle Plan" to real life issues we all face as men by looking closely at some particular surface idols, traps, and behaviors that are motivated by our three deep idols.

II. CONTROL

1. The Deep Idol of CONTROL tells us the fundamental ______________________ that, "if I can just maintain influence or mastery over this situation, people in my life, my performance, my schedule, my income, or whatever... THEN I'll be okay, content, dominate, strong, and safe."

2. Our lust for control can make us men of fear.

3. The Fear Trap

   List of potiental things you can fear:

   - Fears for your safety and the safety of those you love.
   - Fears about how you will die: disease, cancer, being alone, broke, drowning, in a plane crash

[1]The content of this session has been shaped and influenced by Edward T. Welch, *Running Scared: Fear, Worry, and The Rest of God.*

- Fears about what happens after death, being forgotten, judged, extinct
- Fears about living a meaningless life
- Fears about being unloved or alone
- Fears about being in love and then hurt or abandoned
- Fears about what you might lose: a friend, your girlfriend, your hair, your youth, your mind, money, your job, your spouse, your health, your purpose, or even your faith.

From *Running Scared* by Ed Welch[2]

- We can have a Deep Idol of CONTROL to the point that it can overwhelm us with ____________________.
- Even our bodies can showcase our anxiety.

4. The Workaholism Trap

- Having "work" under control gives us the illusion and mirage of ________________________. It makes us think our future is protected.
- The need for CONTROL drives fear, and _______________ can drive workaholism. We are so afraid of not having control that we can't take a break.

5. The Anger Trap

- Fear can make us an ___________________________ person with a short fuse and an explosive, toxic tongue.
- Look behind anger and you will find fear. Look behind fear and you will find CONTROL.

6. The Power Trap

- The power trap is motivated by the ___________________________ to dominate.

[2]See Welch, *Running Scared*, 28.

III. REPLACING IDOLS OF CONTROL- TRUST AND STEWARDSHIP

1. Replacing Fear

    - Fear creates a fork in the road, and we can either turn to or run to ourselves or we can turn to and run to __________________________and His truth and grace.
    - We can replace fear with trust.
    - Let's look at some of the truths of Scripture that will help us remember this and fight the battle against the fear side of CONTROL.
        - "Do you know what the most frequent command in the Bible turns out to be? What instruction, what order, is given, again and again, by God, by angels, by Jesus, by prophets and apostles? What do you think – 'Be good'? 'Be holy'? Or, negatively, 'Don't sin'? 'Don't be immoral'? No. The most frequent command in the Bible is: 'Don't be afraid Don't be afraid. Fear not. Don't be afraid."[3]
          –Biblical Scholar, N. T. Wright
        - "Trust in the Lord with all your heart and do not lean on your own understanding. In all your ways acknowledge him, and He will make straight your paths." Proverbs 3:5 (ESV)
        - Jesus says: "I tell you, do not be anxious about your life, what you will eat or what you will drink, nor about your body, what you will put on...for your heavenly Father knows that you need them all. But seek first the kingdom of God and His righteousness, and all of these things will be added unto you." Matthew 6 (ESV)
        - The Bible tells us to trust God, not ourselves with the details of our lives.
        - "Do not be anxious about anything, but in everything by prayer and supplication with thanksgiving let your requests be made known to God. And the peace of God, which surpasses all understanding, will guard your hearts and your minds in Christ Jesus." Philippians 4:6–7 (ESV)

[3]N.T. Wright, *Following Jesus: Biblical Reflections on Discipleship* (Grand Rapids: Erdmans, 1995), 66.

2. Replacing Power

- One antidote for power is the Biblical concept of ________________________. Things aren't given to us to control or dominate; rather, they are given to us as a stewardship.

- "Biblical stewardship touches every area of our lives. It requires a basic commitment to present ourselves completely to God as His servants, with no strings attached . . . . The ultimate question, then, is this: Am I the lord of my life, or is Christ the Lord of my life? . . . This is the difference between the great 'I will' and the great 'Thy will . . . " A wise STEWARD will treat things according to their true value, treasure the things that God declares to be important and hold with a loose grip the things that God says will not matter in the end."[4] –Ken Boa

IV. CONCLUSION

1. In the next and final session of this volume of *33 the Series*, we will look at the other deep idols: COMFORT and SIGNIFICANCE.

[4]Kenneth Boa, "Stewardship." Online: http://bible.org/seriespage/stewardship.

DISCUSSION / REFLECTION QUESTIONS

1. Several traps can emerge from the deep idol of control: fear, workaholism, anger, and power. Discuss any of these traps that can be a temptation for you.

2. When was the last time that you got really angry? What caused it? Was an idol of yours involved?

3. How should the concept of stewardship change our perspective of the things and the people that God has allowed in our lives?

4. Discuss John Bryson's testimony about his struggle with control. How could you relate?

5. Write down (on page 89) and share with your group your one or two STRATEGIC MOVES that you need to make in order to apply what you've learned in this session.

RESOURCES ON THE FOLLOWING PAGES:

YOU'RE NOT

REVELATION 1:8– "I AM THE ALPHA AND THE OM
LORD GOD, "WHO IS AND WHO WAS AND WHO I
ALMIGHTY." PROVERBS 19:21–"MANY ARE TH
OF THE LORD THAT WILL STAND." ISAIAH 45:6
SUN AND FROM THE WEST, THAT THERE IS NONE
I FORM LIGHT AND CREATE DARKNESS, I MAKE W
DOES ALL THESE THINGS." MATTHEW 19:26–"B
IMPOSSIBLE, BUT WITH GOD ALL THINGS ARE POS
INHERITANCE, HAVING BEEN PREDESTINED ACCO
ACCORDING TO THE COUNSEL OF HIS WILL" PSA
RULES OVER THE NATIONS." JOSHUA 1:9– "HAVE
NOT BE FRIGHTENED, AND DO NOT BE DISMAYED,
JOB 12:10–"IN HIS HAND IS THE LIFE OF EVERY LIVI
"THE KING'S HEART IS A STREAM OF WATER IN T

N CONTROL.

AYS THE
ME, THE

(YOU'RE NOT GOD.)

IN THE MIND OF A MAN, BUT IT IS THE PURPOSE
AT PEOPLE MAY KNOW, FROM THE RISING OF THE
ME; I AM THE LORD, AND THERE IS NO OTHER. 7)
NG AND CREATE CALAMITY, I AM THE LORD, WHO
S LOOKED AT THEM AND SAID, 'WITH MAN THIS IS
EPHESIANS 1:11–"IN HIM WE HAVE OBTAINED AN
THE PURPOSE OF HIM WHO WORKS ALL THINGS
8–"FOR KINGSHIP BELONGS TO THE LORD, AND HE
IMANDED YOU? BE STRONG AND COURAGEOUS. DO
LORD YOUR GOD IS WITH YOU WHEREVER YOU GO."
& THE BREATH OF ALL MANKIND." **PROVERBS 21:1**–
OF THE LORD; HE TURNS IT WHEREVER HE WILL."

BY GUY DELCAMBRE

CONTROL'S Dark Lie

WITHIN EACH OF US LIES A HUNGER, EXISTING ONLY TO BE SATISFIED.

In each day the hunger waits for all that we will offer. For years, it patiently feeds, strengthening in the more given. It is we who give and It that demands. Like a parasite unattended to or unrecognized, It feasts thieving from good parts of us, always demanding a bigger plate and better seat at the table of the heart. The parasitic hunger, though once small and unnoticeable, imposes devilishly and works deviantly for Its own satisfaction.

And what is that hunger within, us always waiting to feed on all that we offer, but Control?

It seems like a buried treasure that must be discovered, found and owned, Control lures us off course into the thickets and trees where we fight to own the moment, to manipulate the circumstance, to master the day and then, finally, all will be well. Yes, at the work of OUR hands, the day will rise.

IT FEEDS ON ALL THAT WE GIVE TO IT. AND IT ALWAYS WANTS MORE.

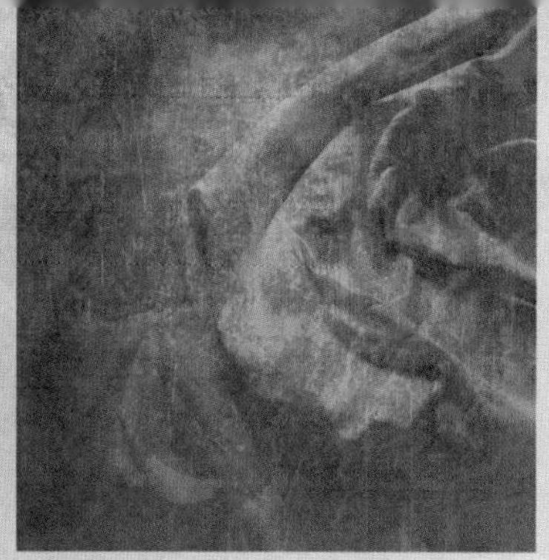

EET BOB.

awoke to complete silence. There was no sunlight, nor birds chirping in warm, calm winds. No aromatic draw n coffee brewing or kids shuffling and stirring. In fact, it still filled the window just near the bed. The alarm k quiet as it should be when all should be sleeping, ceful and mostly not bothered.

its were beginning to bleed into day dimming even the htest and happiest moments where all cause for ease celebration usually exist fittingly. And these infringing ts cannibalistically grew into weeks and months where only place Bob found any semblance of peace was in the er chair, alone, while everyone else slept.

HILE THE OTHERS RESTFULLY VAITED THE NEXT DAY, HE NK SOFTER GROWING OLDER THE CHAIR AT NIGHT, **AWAKE.**

a gregarious man, admirably humble in his approach e, warm to everyone, confident in conversation and in relationships but now, aloof even to those closest to with a growing distance. Everyone loved Bob and the in which he managed career, family, and life. He was sought after by colleagues for advice and perspective, e sign of recognized achievement. And Bob loved hat.

Without proper realization, he clung to and tucked away compliments and pats on his back as signs of not mere affirmation, but pre-deviantly, validation. He swore to be something, to give his family something better than what he had growing up and figuring out patches of life on his own as his dad tirelessly worked for what was hardly ever enough.

Bob was afraid of losing. The more of himself he offered to fear and the less control he held, the more he lost. Fear echoed inside, concealing itself inside of his decisions and leaving space for doubt and insecurity. Now, even the menial decisions and choices that needed to be made throughout the workday haunted him. Friends and colleagues knew him as a stable source, someone found out for advice and encouragement. The future ahead promised much, but now, something specific was not right.

He woke in the middle of night dislodged, close to a whispering voice hinting the possibility of all things right and good spoiling, becoming bad somehow and crumbling wrong. There he sat sunken into the chair in the dimly lit corner fixated by the surrounding good, his wife of 15 years, the lively children nestled in bed, his plateauing career once blooming successful, friends, neighbors and his reputation; all spoiling out of his control.

Something was increasingly not right.

He didn't feel depressed, but diminished, even shrinking, as life moved regularly from day to day. Control and its unending appetite, its tireless desire for more from within tolled on him. Increasingly he hung in moments despondent.

Night after night, Bob woke and worried. Alone he sat fading and fearful, almost ambiguously, about everything. He worked so hard to get to this very point in life where life would shift into easier, more enjoyable days. Bob banked on every one of those long days reaching through family time into evenings. The pay-off always seemed so worth it. One project deadline, another deal to be closed, a pivotal meeting to be held, all in the name of advancement, promotion, security and success. All in

in the spirit of providing well for his family, the ones he could only struggle to describe. Bob knew spreadsheets, reports, statistics, colleagues, competitors, and market trends better than anything else in life. He had to. He had to control and master his ship blown by the wind, the mantra, that life is for the taking to those who will take it. Bob wouldn't fail only to return to the medial cubicle he once occupied tethered to obscurity and lighter pockets.

Years ago now, the first time Bob's boss called him out of his generic cubicle into his office and closed the door, life and all that mattered changed. Bob was noticed, recognized finally for all of his hard work and dedication to the work given to him. Even now, sitting alone at night, again, in the corner chair surrounded by plaques and signs of recognition adorning the walls of his home study, he remembered the first time his boss walked him into the corner office and awarded him. He could recall with ease how his hands clinched the door knob of his new corner office that first time—a sure sign of success and achievement grasped by his own hands.

After hours passed like days, there in the corner chair he suddenly noticed the room brighten a bit. He found his way to the bathroom to ready himself for the day arriving but something within weaned. Slowly, his hand familiarly reached out for the light switch without breaking stride and aimed straight for the sink. Nothing focused into his immediate attention as he grabbed each side of the sink basin leaning forward, shoulders hung low and exhaled heavily. The sound of the mirror compartment snapping shut startled him. Bob stood, bemused, as he peered into the bathroom mirror. Lines cut deep into his face, deeper than he ever recalled and the man he saw looked diminished staring back. He saw himself strangely dim; the reflection eerily didn't mimic his exactness. He rubbed his eyes as an assist to his attempts of gaining clarity and focus. Not only did he increasingly sense himself a foreign fit into his own life, but staring into the mirror he felt alien and nonnative, tossing in waves that were both pushing and pulling him to and from himself.

Bob stared deeply into the eyes weakly looking back, the ones strangely unfamiliar. Lost in the moment a trading of places somehow happened.

ALL ALIVE PARTS OF HIM – HOPES, DREAMS, TRUST, BELONGING – ALL WITHDREW INSIDE AND SUCCUMBED TO **THE FEAR OF LOSING GRIP AND CONTROL.**

Days moved by darker as Bob shuffled through a lesser imprint of himself, a counterfeit following a routine. His ear owned by fear's voice that had matured beyond a small echo inside to the central voice that gave rhythm to his shuffled steps. Like a ball of yarn nraveling revolution by revolution, Bob heeded fear's ıfluence religiously. The more he grasped for control, he more tangled and intertwined he was held. Fear of osing control, achievement, and all evidences of his hands wned his very affection, thieved away from those who oved and admired him most. His eyes filtered decisions nd interactions through insecurity. Bob was no more than puppet, a thing of response to fear.

Ionths gave way to years, a heap of nights alone and wake. Slowly, Bob digressed inwardly more as pictures f him younger and alive only seemed as evidential ccusations of who he couldn't become.

nd then one day, Bob lost incomprehensibly.

e was awake of course this particular night when veryone else was not. Unable to sleep again, he sunk into ıe chair in the corner. Like an altar, the chair grew into ıe place where Bob surrendered and fear mastered him.

he phone rang. He answered to hear news that crashed pon him with the weight of a thousand years.

is son . . . an accident . . . his car . . . hospital . . . fatal.

Sir, are you there?"

'm sorry, what?!"

'our son was involved in an automobile accident. esponders tried all they could, sir, but your son did not ake it. In route to the hospital, they lost him. They will be the hospital momentarily. I need you to come, sir."

ear seized the heart it owned and Bob faded through s he shook the hands of friends and family. The funeral appened. He knew that much, but not much else. Fear ssured him that he could do nothing to hold on to the ings he wanted or loved.

e sank even more than he ever imagined one could. Life darkened dismally, further from rest, deeper in fear; a life-prisoner, chained to a fear that repainted Bob's days even dimmer.

Like a prisoner serving a life sentence, Bob held no hope of anything other than resetting expectations and adapting to conditions restricted. Something extraordinary would have to be done for him to ever see the light of day again.

That something found him in an object that nearly tripped him late one night as he walked into his son's old room. A journal, belonging to his son some years ago, speaking of a man who held the world and fiercely wielded the day as his own. A man of giant-like stature holding all that he loved close, inspiring bravery in the smallest of hearts.

AT THE FOOT OF THE PAGE, A DRAWN IMAGE OF A BOY AND A GIANT—A SON AND HIS FATHER—**BOB.**

In that moment, a forgotten and given-up-on idea in Bob's life surged past all hurt, pain, scars and fear, with a speed undetected. God. Bob was found, not by his own effort or attention, but by Someone he long ago and forever forward vowed to distrust due to disappointments and fear, construing life inverted and perverted from God's reality. A new peace entered his soul. It was OK. He knew it now with all of his heart. God is in control.

Slowly, Bob awoke to a new a day where nights lasted normal, where he was only awakened by the light of a new day. In surrender to God's love and acceptance, Bob returned to much more of who he once was, a man not owned by control and fear of losing, but a man fully trusting that the Creator of the universe, and all that is in it, is much better at being in control than he could ever be.

Thoughts on FEAR

THROUGH THE AGES

- The only thing we have to fear is...fear itself. – Franklin D. Roosevelt
- The enemy is fear. We think it is hate; but, it is fear. – Gandhi
- Fear is the path to the dark side. Fear leads to anger. Anger leads to hate. Hate causes suffering. – Yoda
- If fear is cultivated it will become stronger, if faith is cultivated it will achieve mastery. – John Paul Jones
- Almost everything—all external expectations, all pride, all fear of embarrassment or failure—these things just fall away in the face of death, leaving only what is truly important. – Steve Jobs
- We can easily forgive a child who is afraid of the dark; the real tragedy of life is when men are afraid of the light. – Plato
- The sorrow of God lies in our fear of Him, our fear of life, and our fear of ourselves. He anguishes over our self-absorption and self-sufficiency... God's sorrow lies in our refusal to approach Him when we sinned and failed. – Brennan Manning
- Don't misunderstand me, danger is very real. But fear is a choice. – Will Smith

SCRIPTURE REFERENCES

Proverbs 3:5 (ESV) "Trust in the Lord with all your heart and do not lean on your own understanding. In all your ways acknowledge him, and he will make straight your paths."

Matthew 6:25, 32–33 25 (ESV) "I tell you, do not be anxious about your life, what you will eat or what you will drink, nor about your body, what you will put on . . . for your heavenly Father knows that you need them all. But seek first the kingdom of God and his righteousness, and all of these things will be added unto you."

John 14:1 (ESV) "Let not your hearts be troubled. Believe in God; believe also in me."

1 Peter 5:6–7 (ESV) "Humble yourselves, therefore, under the mighty hand of God so that at the proper time he may exalt you, casting all your anxieties on him, because he cares for you."

Philippians 4:6–7 (ESV) "Do not be anxious about anything, but in everything by prayer and supplication with thanksgiving let your requests be made known to God. And the peace of God, which surpasses all understanding, will guard your hearts and your minds in Christ Jesus."

SUPPORTING RESOURCES

Edward T. Welch. *Running Scared: Fear, Worry, and the God of Rest.* New Growth Press, 2007. This is the best resource available for a more in-depth look at the problem of fear and anxiety. Welch not only provides insightful analysis into the intricacies of fear but also biblical solutions to fight it.

** The content in the resources above does not necessarily reflect the opinion of Authentic Manhood. Readers should utilize these resources but form their own opinions.*

Significance & Comfort

SESSION **SIX** | Training Guide

Significance & Comfort

Presented by Tierce Green

I. INTRODUCTION[1]

1. We laid out a grid of deep idols and gave you an IDOLATRY FRAMEWORK, and we discovered a biblical "Battle Plan" for ____________________________ idols.

II. SIGNIFICANCE

1. The deep idol of SIGNIFICANCE tells us the basic lie that "If a certain person, a certain social group, or the colleagues in my profession... if they find me worthy of attention or love, if they acknowledge my value or greatness, as long as I am not disgraced before them... THEN I'll be important and acceptable."

2. The Approval Trap

   - Also called the "FEAR OF MAN," is often overly concerned with disappointing or upsetting other people.

   - You may be hypersensitive to ___________________________ and often react—even to the slightest criticism—with extreme responses.

   - The approval trap also shows itself in men who are controlled by a need to please a parent.

3. The Recognition Trap

   - The recognition trap is based on pride, hungers for admiration and fame and is often fueled by ___________________________________ with other men.

4. The Relationship Trap

   - Shows up when a man is tempted to feel "less than" if he is not in a relationship.

[1] The content of this session has been shaped and influenced by Edward T. Welch, *When People Are Big and God Is Small: Overcoming Peer Pressure, Codependency, and the Fear of Man* (Phillipsburg: P&R Publishing, 1997).

III. REPLACING THE IDOL OF SIGNIFICANCE

1. In his booklet "Gospel Relationships," author Tim Chester offers one cure for the deep idol of significance.

    - "The answer to the fear of man is the fear of God. We need a big view of God. To fear God is to respect, worship, trust and submit to God. To fear God is to have proper appreciation of His holiness, majesty, glory, power, love and wrath. Christians can now call God our Father, and fear in the sense of 'terror' has been taken away... [We must] meditate on God's glory, greatness, holiness, power, splendor, beauty, grace, mercy, and love. Encourage anyone struggling with fear of man issues to compare the person(s) they fear with God."[2]

    - By fear of God, the Bible doesn't mean terror but REVERENTIAL AWE.

    For more on the Fear of Man, visit the feature in the Training Guide found on page 106-107

2. Another antidote for the Significance Idol is ______________________________

    - Tim Keller, in his booklet on self-forgetfulness, says this:

        - "The thing we remember from meeting a truly gospel-humble person is how much they seem totally interested in us. Because the essence of gospel-humility is not thinking MORE of myself or thinking LESS of myself; it is thinking of myself less."[3]

    - When we TRULY follow what Jesus called the second greatest commandment—the commandment to ________________________ your neighbor as yourself—the importance of our significance fades to the background.

[2] As quoted at http://secondmilechurch.wordpress.com/2011/01/18/the-antidote-to-fearing-man-people-pleasing/. Chester makes a similar point in his recent book, *Everyday Church: Gospel Communities on Mission* (Wheaton: Crossway, 2012), 76–80
[3] Timothy Keller, *The Freedom of Self-Forgetfulness: The Path to True Christian Joy* (Chorley: 10 Publishing, 2012).

IV. COMFORT

1. The Deep Idol of COMFORT tells us the lie that, "If I can just maintain physical ease or relaxation, if I can just be laid back, if I can just keep from stress or responsibility and experience some pleasure and enjoyment, then life will be more fulfilling, easy, fun, or thrilling."

2. The Fear of Responsibility Trap

   - When a man hides from obligation, believing that real happiness is found APART from responsibility.

3. The Dependence on Consumption Trap

   - The preoccupation with consumption is a diversion, but it's not a solution to the stressful messes around them.

4. The Turning to Escapes Trap

   - When a man turns to illegitimate outlets to escape the harshness or pain of his life and find relief.

V. REPLACING THE IDOL OF COMFORT

1. "The pleasure of life comes not in the pursuit of pleasure but in the fulfillment of responsibility."

    - "Godly ______________________________" is the desire to achieve something for the glory of God.

2. The ultimate antidote for all idols is God.

VI. CONCLUSION

1. To worship idols and fall for the traps they produce is to ______________________________ the living waters God offers in exchange for broken cisterns that do not hold water.

2. Idols do not work for us: they leave us thirstier and more desperate.

3. Like Jesus, Authentic Men are a ______________________________- giving spirit, who lead courageously and invest eternally.

DISCUSSION/ REFLECTION QUESTIONS

1. Which of the significance traps is most relevant for you: the approval trap, the recognition trap, or the relationship trap? Discuss.

2. Which of the comfort traps is most relevant for you: the fear of responsibility, the dependence on consumption, or turning to escapes? Discuss.

3. How did Tierce sharing about his comfort idol speak to you? What are some things you could "miss out on" if you bow to the idol of comfort?

4. Do you think of "ambition" as a good thing or a bad thing? Discuss the difference between "ambition" and "Godly ambition."

5. Remember to take time to write out a Strategic Move for this session and also to transfer all of your strategic moves into an Action Plan using the chart on page 115.

RESOURCES ON THE FOLLOWING PAGES:

FEAR OF MAN

Straight from the lies of Significan

"THE ANSWER TO THE FEAR OF MAN IS THE FEAR OF GOD. We need a big view of God. To fear God is to respect, worship, trust and submit to God. To fear God is to have a proper appreciation of his holiness, majesty, glory, power, love and wrath. Christians can now call God our Father, and fear in the sense of 'terror' has been taken away...[We must] meditate on God's glory, greatness, holiness, power, splendor, beauty, grace, mercy and love. Encourage anyone struggling with fear of man issues to compare the person(s) they fear with God." *Gospel Relationships* – **TIM CHESTER**

THE FOLLOWING QUESTIONS will help you determine if a idol of significance manifest itself in your life through "fear of man" issues:

- Are you constantly preoccupied with keeping everybody happy?
- Is the possibility of disappointing others lethal to your contentment?
- Are you afraid of saying no and setting boundaries?
- Do you find your schedule overstuffed in an effort to please others?
- Does the thought of having to confront others with a hard fact or truth make you nauseous?
- Do you have a tendency to avoid telling people what you really think?
- Are you always softening your real opinions to make them more palatable for others?
- Do you struggle with a low self-esteem?
- Do you avoid public settings or leadership opportunities because of the potential for failure?
- Are you constantly managing people's perceptions of you even if it means spinning the facts when necessary?

Anytime you have fear of MAN issues you need to compare MAN with God:

NATURE OF MAN:

Created
Sinful
Conditional love
Judgmental
Self-focused
Selfish
Needs leading
Prideful
Desire of power
Not in control
Insecure
Inconsistent
Desire of comfort
Limited
Not always right
Confused

NATURE OF GOD:

Creator
Perfect
Always Right
Unconditional love
Eternally steadfast
Powerful
Merciful
Unparalled
Unprecedented
Preeminent
Indescribable
Incomprehensible
Grace is sufficient
Rewards the diligent
Sovereign
Trustworthy
Supreme

[ROMANS 7:15, 18-20, 24]

I REALLY DONT UNDERSTAND ::MYSELF::

FOR I WANT TO DO WHAT IS RIGHT, BUT I DONT DO IT. INSTEAD, I DO WHAT I HATE. AND I KNOW THAT NOTHING GOOD LIVES IN ME, THAT IS, IN MY SINFUL NATURE. I WANT TO DO WHAT IS RIGHT, BUT I CANT. I WANT TO DO WHAT IS GOOD, BUT I DONT. I DONT WANT TO DO WHAT IS WRONG, BUT I DO IT ANYWAY. BUT IF I DO WHAT I DONT WANT TO DO, I AM REALLY THE ONE DOING WRONG; IT IS SIN LIVING IN ME THAT DOES IT. OH, WHAT A MISERABLE PERSON I AM!

WHO WILL FREE ME FROM THIS THAT IS DOMINA ::BY SIN&DEATH?

[ROMANS 7:25 & 8:1-2]

THANK GOD!

* THE ANSWER IS IN JESUS CHRIST OUR LORD.

SO YOU SEE HOW IT IS: IN MY MIND I REALLY WANT TO OBEY GOD'S LAW, BUT BECAUSE OF MY SINFUL NATURE I AM A SLAVE TO SIN... SO NOW THERE IS NO CONDEMNATION FOR THOSE WHO BELONG TO CHRIST JESUS. AND BECAUSE YOU BELONG TO HIM, THE POWER OF THE LIFE-GIVING SPIRIT HAS FREED YOU FROM THE POWER OF SIN THAT LEADS TO DEATH.

MUCH ADO ABOUT NOTHING

VAIN ATTEMPTS FOR SIGNIFICANCE

When men turn their God-given energy and passion toward pursuits of no lasting value, the resul can be disastrous, comical…and downright sad. Here are a handful of accomplishments by the male version of the species that might best be categorized as " scratchers." And as absurd as they may be, in comparison to more socially accepted pursuits, they ma end up leading to the same place—a dead end.

the RED ZONE

- Irish artist Frank Buckley built an actual house out of 1.4 billion shredded, decommissioned euros (US $2.3 billion). The three-room house, comprised of a living room, bedroom, and a bathroom, was intended as a statement about the madness of the global economic collapse. Says Buckley: "Whatever you say about the euro, it's a great insulator"(billioneurohouse.com)

- Glynn Wolfe, a California resident, set the world record for most monogamous marriages by being married to 29 different women. The longest of his marriages lasted eleven years; the shortest was 19 days. Twenty-four of his marriages ended in divorce; four ended because of the death of his wife. The 29th marriage ended with his own death at age 89.

- Niek Vermeulen of the Netherlands has collected 6,016 unique airline sickness bags from 1,142 different airlines from more than 160 countries. Niek began collecting the bags—all unused—in the 1970s after making a bet with a friend to see who could collect the most of one item (Niek won). His favorite is an airsickness bag from NASA's space shuttle Columbia.

- Takeru Kobayashi set his first eating world record in his rookie appearance at the Nathan's Coney Island hot dog-eating contest, consuming 50 hot dogs in 12 minutes. He would top that record three more times. Kobayashi also holds the record for eating 17.7 pounds of cow brains in 15 minutes; 58 bratwurst sausages in ten minutes; 14 Twinkies in one minute; and 337 hot wings in one sitting. Kobayashi weighs only 128 pounds.

- Okan Kaya played the video game Call of Duty for 135 straight hours, setting the world record for marathon gaming. Kaya was allowed only brief, periodic breaks each hour to rest or catch a moment of sleep. "My hands were cramping up and I went through a lot of bandages," Kaya explains. Kaya also occasionally used a small Stair Master while he was playing to prevent potentially fatal blood clots.

- Upon retiring from a 30-year teaching career, Dave Moffitt embarked on an epic road trip that allowed him to see every NFL, AFL, NHL, MLB, MLS, NBA, WNBA, CBA and NBDL team play at its home stadium or arena (including baseball spring training sites), as well as NASCAR races, pro golf tournaments, hundreds of horse races, high school, college and even Little League games. Moffitt sleeps in his car and travels alone. "I like being by myself," he says. "I taught kids for 34 years. I've heard enough."

SCRIPTURE REFERENCES

Jeremiah 2:13 (ESV) “My people have committed two evils: they have forsaken me, the fountain of living waters, and hewed out cisterns for themselves, broken cisterns that can hold no water.”

Jeremiah 17:5–8 (ESV) Thus says the LORD: “Cursed is the man who trusts in man and makes flesh his strength, whose heart turns away from the LORD. He is like a shrub in the desert, and shall not see any good come. He shall dwell in the parched places of the wilderness, in an uninhabited salt land. Blessed is the man who trusts in the LORD, whose trust is the LORD. He is like a tree planted by water, that sends out its roots by the stream, and does not fear when heat comes, for its leaves remain green, and is not anxious in the year of drought, for it does not cease to bear fruit.”

John 4:34 (ESV) Jesus said to them, “My food is to do the will of him who sent me and to accomplish his work.”

Colossians 3:23 (ESV) “Whatever you do, work heartily, as for the Lord and not for men.”

SUPPORTING RESOURCES

Harvey, Dave. *Rescuing Ambition*. Crossway, 2010. Dave Harvey argues that the concept of “ambition” has often gotten a bad rap. Harvey maintains that, when put to work for the glory of God, ambition can be quite useful and pious.

Keller, Tim. *Self-Forgetfulness: The Path to True Christian Joy*. 10Publishing, 2012. In this small booklet, Tim Keller urges readers away from self-love and self-hate and toward “self-forgetfulness” as the path to real freedom and joy.

Packer, J. I. *Knowing God*. InterVarsity Press, 1993. A great way to combat fear of man is with the fear of God. In *Knowing God*, Packer outlines the major attributes of God’s character. This book will help you know God better and build your awe and wonder of Him.

Welch, Edward T. *When People Are Big and God is Small: Overcoming Peer Pressure, Codependency, and the Fear of Man*. P&R Publising, 1997. This book is probably the best place to start to understand and battle the “approval trap” and the “fear of man.”

**The content in the resources above does not necessarily reflect the opinion of Authentic Manhood. Readers should utilize these resources but form their own opinions.*

ACTION PLAN

YOUR STRATEGIC MOVE | SESSION ONE : **IDOLS**

____

____

YOUR STRATEGIC MOVE | SESSION TWO : **EMPTY PROMISES**

____

____

YOUR STRATEGIC MOVE | SESSION THREE : **BATTLE PLAN**

____

____

YOUR STRATEGIC MOVE | SESSION FOUR : **XXX**

____

____

YOUR STRATEGIC MOVE | SESSION FIVE : **CONTROL**

____

____

YOUR STRATEGIC MOVE | SESSION SIX : **SIGNIFICANCE & COMFORT**

____

____

ADDITIONAL

THE PURSUIT OF HOLINESS By Jerry Bridges

The Pursuit of Holiness *helps us see clearly just what we should rely on God to do--and what we should take responsibility for ourselves.*

EXPLICT GOSPEL By Matt Chandler

Inspired by the needs of both the overchurched and the unchurched, and bolstered by the common neglect of the explicit gospel within Christianity, popular pastor Matt Chandler writes this punchy treatise to remind us what is of first and utmost importance—the gospel.

COUNTERFEIT GODS By Tim Keller

In this inspiring new book, Timothy Keller, reveals the unvarnished truth about faith, our hearts' desires, and the pursuit of happiness- and where all of it can ultimately be found.

HOW PEOPLE CHANGE By Tim Lane and Paul Tripp

Change involves more than a biblical formula: you will see how God is at work to make you the person you were created to be. That powerful, loving, redemptive relationship is at the heart of all positive change you experience.

RUNNING SCARED- FEAR, WORRY, AND THE REST OF GOD By Edward T. Welch

In his new release, Running Scared, *Edward T. Welch investigates the roots of fear in the human soul and the ramifications of living in the grips of anxiety, worry, and dread. Welch encourages readers to discover for themselves that the Bible is full of beautiful words of comfort for fearful people (and that every single person is afraid of something).*

THE FREEDOM OF SELF-FORGETFULNES by Timothy Keller

In this short and punchy book, best selling author Timothy Keller shows that gospel humility means we can stop connecting every experience, every conversation with ourselves and can thus be free from self condemnation. A truly gospel humble person is not a self hating person or a self loving person, but a self forgetful person.

BREAKING THE IDOLS OF YOUR HEART- HOW TO NAVIGATE TEMPTATIONS OF LIFE By Dan Allender

In Breaking the Idols of Your Heart- How to Navigate Temptations of Life, *Dan Allender and Tremper Longman illuminate for us the Teacher in Ecclesiastes warnings and, after all his activities, his final radiant conclusion: Meaning and purpose come only when God is truly the center of our life and the object of our hope.*

JESUS + NOTHING = EVERYTHING By Tullian Tchividjian

It's so easy to forget what the Christian faith is all about. We struggle so much, work so hard, and fail so often that we frequently sense something in the equation of life must be missing.
Ultimately, Tchividjian reminds us that Jesus is the whole of the equation as he boldly proclaims that Jesus plus nothing really is everything.

HAZARDS OF BEING A MAN By Jeffery E. Miller

Jeffrey E. Miller challenges men to acknowledge their common struggles and weaknesses to help them become better men.

THE HOLE IN OUR HOLINESS By Kevin DeYoung

This is a book for those of us who are ready to take holiness seriously, ready to be more like Jesus, ready to live in light of the grace that produces godliness. This is a book about God's power to help us grow in personal holiness and to enjoy the process of transformation.

RESOURCES

GODS AT WAR- DEFEATING THE IDOLS THAT BATTLE YOUR HEART BY KYLE IDLEMAN

In Gods at War, *Kyle Idleman, bestselling author of* Not a Fan, *helps every believer recognize there are false gods at war within each of us, and they battle for the place of glory and control in our lives. What keeps us from truly following Jesus is that our hearts are pursuing something or someone else. Using true, powerful and honest testimonies of those who have struggled in each area, gods at war illustrates a clear path away from the heartache of our 21st century idolatry back to the heart of God—enabling us to truly be completely committed followers of Jesus.*

SHAME INTERRUPTED- HOW GOD LIFTS THE PAIN OF WORTHLESSNESS AND REJECTION BY EDWARD T. WELCH

Shame controls far too many of us. But the Bible is about shame from start to finish, and, if we are willing, God's beautiful words break through. Look at Jesus through the lens of shame and see how the marginalized and worthless are his favorites and become his people. God cares for the shamed. Through Jesus you are covered, adopted, cleansed, and healed.

GALATIANS FOR YOU- FOR READING, FOR FEEDING, FOR LEADING BY TIM KELLER

Galatians For You *is a new curriculum tool you can use to learn or teach from the book of Galatians. Both student and teacher can use it to walk through Galatians, learning how the gospel message changes the whole of our lives.*

WHEN PEOPLE ARE BIG AND GOD IS SMALL BY EDWARD T. WELCH

Overly concerned about what people think of you? Welch uncovers the spiritual dimension of people-pleasing and points the way through a true knowledge of God, ourselves, and others.

RESPECTABLE SINS BY JERRY BRIDGES

Jerry Bridges addresses the "acceptable" sins that we tend to tolerate in ourselves, including pride and anger. He goes to the heart of the matter, exploring our feelings of shame and grief and opening a new door to God's forgiveness and grace.

THE SCREWTAPE LETTERS BY C.S. LEWIS

In this humorous and perceptive exchange between two devils, C. S. Lewis delves into moral questions about good vs. evil, temptation, repentance, and grace. Through this wonderful tale, the reader emerges with a better understanding of what it means to live a faithful life.

ADDICTIONS- A BANQUET TO THE GRAVE BY EDWARD T. WELCH

A worship disorder: this is how Edward T. Welch views addictions. "Will we worship our own desires or will we worship the true God?" With this lens the author discovers far more in Scripture on addictions than passages on drunkenness. Can we not escape our addictions? If we're willing to follow Jesus, the author says that we have "immense hope: hope in God's forgiving grace, hope in God's love that is faithful even when we are not, and hope that God can give power so that we are no longer mastered by the addiction."

** The content in the resources recommended above does not necessarily reflect the opinion of Authentic Manhood. Readers should utilize these resources but form their own opinions.*

A Man and His Traps - Answer Key

SESSION ONE: IDOLS

I. 1. *sin*
II. 2. *struggle*
3. *done*
4.
- *behavior*

III. 1. *heart*
2.
- *good*
- *lie*

3.
- *dominance*
- *humiliation*
- *Pleasure*

SESSION TWO: EMPTY PROMISES

I. 2. *roots*
5. *best*
II. 2. *better*
III. 4.
- *pleasure*

6.
- *significance*

9.
- *God*

IV.
- *duty*

V. 1. *alone*
3. *worship*

SESSION THREE: BATTLE PLAN

I. 1. *idols*
3. *redirected*
5. *misplaced*
II. 2. *replace*
IV. 1.
- *idol*
- *grace*

2.
- *happiness*

3.
- *grace*
- *replace*

V. 1.
- *Comfort*
- *Significance*
- *Control*

2. *promises*
VI. 1.
- *you're*

2.
- *easy*

VII. 1. *for*
2.
iii. *Replace*

SESSION FOUR: XXX

I. *1. lust*

3. accessibility

II. *1.*

- *delight*
- *push*
- *alone*

2.

- *intimacy*

III. *1. honesty*

2. promises

3.

- *satisfying*

IV. *1. intimacy*

4. Jesus

SESSION FIVE: CONTROL

II. *1. lie*

- *fear*

4.

- *security*
- *control*

5.

- *angry*

6.

- *desire*

III. *1.*

- *God*

2.

- *stewardship*

SESSION SIX: SIGNIFICANCE & COMFORT

I. *1. replacing*

II. *2.*

- *criticism*

3.

- *comparison*

III. *2. Self-forgetfulness*

- *love*

V. *1.*

- *ambition*

VI. *1. ignore*

3. life